Estimating Causal Effects Using Experimental and Observational Designs

A Think Tank White Paper

The Governing Board of the
American Educational Research Association
Grants Program

Barbara Schneider
Martin Carnoy
Jeremy Kilpatrick
William H. Schmidt
Richard J. Shavelson

American Educational Research Association
Washington, D.C.
www.aera.net

American Educational Research Association
1430 K Street, NW
Suite 1200
Washington, D.C. 20005

Notice: This report was prepared under the auspices of the American Educational Research Association (AERA) Grants Program with funds from the U.S. Department of Education's National Center for Education Statistics (NCES), of the Institute of Education Sciences, and from the National Science Foundation (NSF) under NSF Grants REC-9980573 and REC-0310268.

International Standard Book Number 0-935302-34-4

Additional copies of this report are available from the American Educational Research Association, 1430 K Street, NW, Suite 1200, Washington, D.C. 20005, www.aera.net

This report is also available online at www.aera.net

Printed in the United States of America

Suggested citation: Schneider, B., Carnoy, M., Kilpatrick, J., Schmidt, W. H., & Shavelson, R. J. (2007). *Estimating causal effects using experimental and observational designs* (report from the Governing Board of the American Educational Research Association Grants Program). Washington, DC: American Educational Research Association.

Cover photograph by Melissa Ricquier/stock.xchng

About the American Educational Research Association

The American Educational Research Association (AERA) is the national interdisciplinary research association for approximately 25,000 scholars who undertake research in education. Founded in 1916, the AERA aims to advance knowledge about education, to encourage scholarly inquiry related to education, and to promote the use of research to improve education and serve the public good. AERA is dedicated to strengthening education research by promoting research of the highest quality, undertaking education and training programs, and advancing sound research and science policy. The Association publishes six peer-reviewed journals and research and methodology books central to the field. Also, AERA offers courses, small grants, and dissertation and postdoctoral training initiatives supported by federal research agencies and private foundations.

About the AERA Grants Program

The AERA Grants Program was established in 1990 with funding from the National Science Foundation (NSF) and the National Center for Education Statistics (NCES). The program seeks to support and develop a strong research infrastructure to assist the nation in realizing its education goals and respond to the growing need for scientific education research related to policy and practice. Through competitive small grants, fellowships, and training components, the program has supported and encouraged researchers from a variety of disciplines (e.g., education, psychology, sociology, economics) to conduct such research using quantitative methods with data from the rich, often longitudinal, datasets sponsored by NSF, NCES, and other federal research agencies.

Contents

Preface   i

1. Introduction   1

2. Causality: Forming an Evidential Base   9

The Logic of Causal Inference 10

The Formal Specification of the Causal
Inference Model 13

Criteria for Making Causal Inferences 16

Causal Relativity 17

Causal Manipulation 17

Temporal Ordering 17

Elimination of Alternative Explanations 18

Issues in the Design and Fielding of
Randomized Experiments 18

Sampling Imbalances 18

Specific Versus Average Effects 19

Atypical Responses 20

Implementing Randomized Assignment 21

Detecting Treatment Effects 26

Additional Design Issues 30

Fielding Randomized Experiments in
Educational Settings 32

3. **Estimating Causal Effects Using Observational Data** 38

Methods for Approximating Randomized Assignment 42

Fixed Effects Models 42

Instrumental Variables 46

Propensity Scores 49

Regression Discontinuity 52

Implications of These Results for Causal Inference 54

4. **Analysis of Large-Scale Datasets: Examples of NSF-Supported Research** 58

Case I. An Experiment With Random Assignment: "How Large Are Teacher Effects?" 59

Research Question and Theoretical Frame 60

Problems With Studies of Teacher Effectiveness 61

Experimental Design: Avoiding Problems of Selection Bias 62

Study Design, Data, and Approach 63

Analyses and Results 64

Implications for Estimating Causal Effects 67

Case II. Approximating a Randomized Experiment: "Effects of Kindergarten Retention Policy on Children's Cognitive Growth in Reading and Mathematics" 69

Research Questions and Theoretical Frame 69

Problems With Studies of Retention 70

Controlling for Selection Bias: Propensity Score Matching 73

Study Design, Data, and Approach 74

Analyses and Results 75

Implications for Estimating Causal Effects 78

Case III. Structural Modeling: *Why Schools Matter: A Cross-National Comparison of Curriculum and Learning* 79

    Research Questions and Theoretical Frame 80

    Problems With Research on Curriculum and Learning 81

    Modeling the Potential Causal Effects of Curriculum on Student Learning 82

    Study Design, Data, and Approach 84

    Analyses and Results 86

    Implications for Estimating Causal Effects 89

Case IV. A Standard Analytic Approach: "The Role of Gender and Friendship in Advanced Course-Taking" 90

    Research Questions and Theoretical Frame 91

    Limitations of Previous Research on Peer Influences 92

    Identifying Potential Causal Effects Using Conventional Statistical Techniques 93

    Study Design, Data, and Approach 95

    Analyses and Results 97

    Implications for Estimating Causal Effects 99

5. Conclusions and Recommendations   109

Forming an Evidential Base With Observational Designs 110

Assessing the Relative Strengths of Experimental and Quasi-Experimental Designs 113

Sustaining a Program of Evidential Research 116

References   120

Biographical Sketches   139

Preface

THIS REPORT ORIGINATED from conversations among members of the Governing Board of the American Educational Research Association (AERA) Grants Program (hereafter referred to as the Grants Board) regarding the strengths and limitations of analyses of large-scale datasets for drawing causal inferences that can inform educational policy. In light of recent attention to the importance of randomized controlled experiments for establishing causal relationships, the Grants Board was concerned that the value of analyses of large-scale datasets for addressing causal questions might be underestimated. To gain a clearer understanding of the logic of causal inference, and the contributions of both randomized controlled experiments and analyses of large-scale datasets in establishing causal relationships, the Grants Board decided to prepare a report that would provide researchers and funding agencies with guidelines for evaluating various methods and analytic approaches for drawing causal inferences.

Consisting of representatives from diverse fields and disciplines of research, the Grants Board was established in 1990 to enhance capacity for conducting quantitative analyses of national and international datasets that have implications for educational policy, with a special emphasis on science and mathematics. The Board funds pre- and postdoctoral fellows as well as researchers pursuing questions regarding the effects of instruction and curricula, organizational practices and policies, and teacher development on student learning, achievement, and educational attainment. Special grants are also awarded to researchers engaged in methodological projects such as the construction of items and scales, reliability of scores, and new approaches to analyzing various outcomes. More than 600 investigators have been funded, and their work appears in leading peer-reviewed journals in education, economics, psychology, and sociology (Whiteley, Seelig, Weinshenker, & Schneider, 2002).

Another activity of the Grants Board is to convene "think tank" meetings. These meetings have been organized at the request of the Board's funders, the National Science Foundation (NSF) and the National Center for Education Statistics (NCES), as a forum for discussing pressing substantive and methodological issues regarding the design and analysis of large-scale studies with key outside experts. As a consequence of several conversations and meetings over a 2-year period with NSF, it was decided to hold a think tank meeting on causal inference.

The purpose of this meeting was to review the usefulness of analyses of observational data for addressing causal questions, as well as to assist NSF in the development of its research portfolio, including guidelines for future solicitations and reviews of existing projects. In preparation for the meeting, it was decided by the Board that it would be useful for a subcommittee to write a report to be critiqued by leading methodologists. This document, written by the Grants Board subcommittee, was discussed at the think tank meeting held at Stanford University on September 28–29, 2005. The first author of this report chaired the subcommittee.

In addition to the authors of this report, participants at the think tank meeting included Juergen Baumert, Anthony Bryk, Eric Hanushek, Paul Holland, James Kemple, Susanna Loeb, Jeanie Murdock, Sean Reardon, Donald Rubin, Gerald Sroufe, and Larry Suter. We thank them all for their thoughtful comments and suggestions for revisions. We also thank the authors of several studies cited in the paper for their comments and suggestions: Joshua Angrist, Robert Bifulco, Janet Currie, Brian Jacob, Spyros Konstantopoulos, Stephen Raudenbush, and Catherine Riegle-Crumb. We especially thank Donald Rubin for his thoughtful review of several earlier drafts of the paper. Thanks also to Steven Haider for his comments on an earlier draft.

A draft of this report was sent to two blind reviewers who made excellent suggestions for revising the manuscript. Felice Levine, AERA Executive Director and member of the Governing Board, presided over this final independent review process. The reviewers later identified themselves; we owe special thanks to George Bohrnstedt and Thomas Cook.

Several AERA Grants Board members, who are not authors of this report, need to be acknowledged and thanked for their contributions, including Stephen Raudenbush[1] and Larry Suter. We also thank Gerald Sroufe and Jerry Pine[2] of the AERA Grants Board for their very helpful comments on earlier drafts of this report. Finally, we wish to thank Lisa Hoogstra, Research Associate at Learning Points Associates, who contributed significantly to the development of this manuscript. It could not have been written without her.

Barbara Schneider
Martin Carnoy
Jeremy Kilpatrick
William H. Schmidt
Richard J. Shavelson[3]

Preface Notes

1 Stephen Raudenbush served on the Grants Board from March 2000 to July 2004.

2 Jerry Pine served on the Grants Board from February 1992 to September 2006.

3 Richard J. Shavelson served on the Grants Board from January 1990 to October 2004.

1. Introduction

AMONG EDUCATIONAL LEADERS AND POLICYMAKERS there has been increasing concern regarding the need for scientifically based evidence on which to base funding decisions for specific educational programs and practices. This concern is fundamentally about having better evidence for making decisions about what programs and practices do or do not work. The need for such evidence leads to causal questions, such as whether particular programs and practices improve student academic achievement, social development, and educational attainment. Issues of causality are not new to the academy or public debate and have a rich history in disciplines such as psychology and philosophy and in specialized fields of education research. Nonetheless, among researchers there is a lack of clarity regarding which designs, methods, and analytic approaches are most appropriate for making causal inferences. This report is intended to help researchers, educators, and policymakers understand causal estimation by describing the logic of causal inference and reviewing designs and methods that allow researchers to draw causal inferences about the effectiveness of educational interventions.

Recently, questions of causality have been at the forefront of educational debates and discussions, in part because of dissatisfaction with the quality of education research and recent federal initiatives designed to promote the accumulation of scientific evidence in education that rely on randomized controlled trials (RCTs). A common concern expressed by those deeply engaged with the educational enterprise, as well as those outside education, revolves around the design of and methods used in education research, which many claim have resulted in fragmented and often unreliable findings (Kaestle, 1993; Levin & O'Donnell, 1999; Sroufe, 1997). Pointing to lack of replication, inappropriate designs for assessing causal effects, and crude analytic procedures, some researchers have argued that it is difficult to accumulate a knowledge base that has value for practice or future study (Cook, 2002; Lagemann, 1999, 2000; Shavelson & Berliner, 1988; Weiss, 1999). Education researchers have long struggled with the need to balance "pure" research with the discovery of "what works" and to evaluate the strengths and weaknesses of various methodologies for addressing particular research questions. Several new national initiatives have brought these issues of methodological rigor to the forefront.

First, The No Child Left Behind Act of 2001 (NCLB) provided a specific definition of scientifically based research and set aside funding for education research studies consistent with that definition. Second, funded research programs in the Institute of Education Sciences (IES), the National Science Foundation (NSF), and the National Institute of Child Health and Human Development (NICHD) have increased calls for intervention studies that provide clear evidence of student learning (for details of this history see Eisenhart & Towne, 2003). Third, projects undertaken by the National Academy of Sciences' National Research Council (NRC) have produced a series of reports focused on improving the quality of education research (see, e.g., NRC, 2002, 2004a).

Evidence-based research is one of the four pillars of NCLB, which places special emphasis on determining, through rigorous scientific study, which educational programs and practices are effective. This concept was reinforced by the Education Sciences Reform Act of 2002, which replaced the Office of Educational Research and Improvement with the newly created IES. The goal of IES is "the transformation of education into an evidence-based field in which decision makers routinely seek out the best available research and data before adopting programs or practices that will affect significant numbers of students" (IES, http://www.ed.gov/about/offices/list/ies/index.html?src=oc). This legislation states that by conducting scientifically based research studies that apply rigorous, systematic, and objective methodology to obtain reliable and valid knowledge, it is possible to identify educational practices and activities that result in improved student learning.

These goals were reiterated in a statement from the Secretary of Education in the *Federal Register* (2005), which noted that "random assignment and quasi-experimental designs [are considered] to be the most rigorous methods to address the question of project effectiveness" (p. 3586). While these designs have particular importance for programs authorized by NCLB and IES, they are also being established as a priority for all U.S. Department of Education programs.

The press for randomized controlled trials is illustrated by the What Works Clearinghouse, a federally funded organization that reviews results of randomized trials that have demonstrated beneficial causal relationships between educational interventions and student outcomes, such as improving early reading comprehension and reducing high school dropout rates. Guided by a technical advisory panel, the What Works Clearinghouse has established quality standards to review available research, placing a high priority on randomized field trials, which are seen as being "among the most appropriate research designs for identifying the impact or effect of an education program or practice" (What Works Clearinghouse, http://www.w-w-c.org). Acknowledging that randomized field trials are not feasible in certain situations or for some research questions, the What Works Clearinghouse also advocates the use of quasi-experiments, that is, comparative studies that carefully attempt to isolate the effect of an intervention through means other than randomization.

IES and other federal agencies have made the use of randomized controlled trials a research priority, and several large-scale studies are currently under way. In addition, NSF, IES, and NICHD have collaborated in sponsoring the Interagency Education Research Initiative (IERI), a program that is explicitly designed to bring promising educational interventions to scale. The program promotes research that identifies promising interventions through rigorous randomized trials; when there are justifiable results, it in turn supports the replication of interventions with other groups of participants. To date, the IERI has approximately 108 projects either in the developmental testing phase of an intervention or in the process of bringing an intervention to scale (McDonald, Keesler, Kauffman, & Schneider, 2006; Schneider & McDonald, 2007a, 2007b).

Another program designed to review evidence-based research in education has been undertaken by the NRC, the operating arm of the National Academies. In 2000, NRC established a committee to "review and synthesize recent literature on the science and practice of scientific educational research and consider how to support high-quality science in a federal education research agency" (NRC, 2002, p. 22). The committee, composed of scholars with diverse disciplinary affiliations and varied methodological expertise, carried out several activities aimed at identifying what constitutes scientific research and how the principles of science can be translated into education research. The committee published the monograph *Scientific Research in Education* (NRC, 2002), which provides an articulation of what constitutes high-quality scientific inquiry in education. A follow-up committee produced a second report, *Advancing Scientific Research in Education* (NRC, 2004a), which recommends ways to promote evidence-based research in education.

The two committees concluded that, when financially, logistically, and ethically feasible, the randomized field trial is the best design for making causal inferences about the effectiveness of educational programs and practices. However, they also emphasized that random assignment is not always warranted, feasible, or ethical and recommend the use of quasi-experiments and statistical modeling in these instances.[4]

The NRC maintained that one way to shape the understanding of what constitutes high-quality scientific research is to create and sustain a set of norms and common discourse in the educational community regardless of methodological differences (see also Feuer, Towne, & Shavelson, 2002). To this end, the first committee outlined a set of six guiding principles that it concluded should underlie all scientific inquiry. These principles formed the core of *Scientific Research in Education* (NRC, 2002), which continues to have a significant influence both nationally and internationally among scientists in education and other fields. (Both *Educational Researcher* and *Teachers College Record* have published theme issues on it ["Scientific research," 2002; "Scientific research," 2005]; also see Giangreco & Taylor, 2003; Horner, Carr, Halle, McGee, Odom, & Wolery, 2005; Kamil, 2004; Lagemann, 2005; Levin, 2003; Mayer, 2003; Rover, 2005; Stoiber, 2002; Thompson, Diamond, McWilliam, Snyder, & Snyder, 2005.)[5]

Consensus on these guidelines has not been reached within the education research community. There are a number of researchers who are at odds with the philosophical and methodological value placed on scientific principles as a basis for understanding the implications and consequences of educational reforms for students and their teachers (Bloch, 2004;

Fish, 2003; Gee, 2005; Lather, 2004; Moss, 2005; Popkewitz, 2004; Spooner & Browder, 2003; Willinsky, 2005). Despite these concerns, the report has become a catalyst for discussion and action in schools and colleges of education and among scholars and policymakers in the NRC and the federal government, primarily because of its clear message regarding what should and should not be considered scientific evidence.

The NRC reports represent instances where diverse independent committees have stated that designs and methods for conducting education research are not equally suitable for addressing particular questions. The committees concluded that research designs should be carefully selected and implemented to best address the question being studied. Not only do certain problems require different designs, but more important, "some methods are better than others for particular purposes, and scientific inferences are constrained by the type of design employed" (NRC, 2002, p. 98).

Recognizing the need to develop criteria for determining which designs and methods are most appropriate for addressing causal questions, NSF has undertaken a systematic review of its education research portfolio with the goal of developing funding guidelines for future solicitations. To assist the agency in this effort, NSF enlisted the support of the AERA Grants Board to evaluate various research designs and their appropriateness for making causal inferences. Specifically, NSF charged the Grants Board with

> (1) defining causal effects, highlighting the strengths and weaknesses of various study designs intended to examine such effects, and describing analytic methods for estimating effects with different types of study designs; (2) reviewing and selecting NSF-supported studies that demonstrate "scientifically-based research" in which appropriate causal inferences are made; and (3) identifying criteria for designing future studies addressing causal effects. (Memorandum, October 6, 2003)

This charge is consistent with the concern of the AERA Grants Board that education researchers become aware of the strengths and weaknesses of various designs and methods for addressing causal questions. In responding to NSF's charge, the present report describes and exemplifies the role of causal inference in providing evidence on the effectiveness of educational programs and practices. Section 2 begins by defining cause and effect and then reviews the logic of causal inference, presents a formal specification of the causal inference model used in randomized controlled experiments, and provides criteria for making such inferences. Section 3 describes alternative designs that have been developed to approximate randomized experiments. Section 4 summarizes four NSF-supported studies that vary in design and methods of analysis. The strengths and limitations of these designs for making causal inferences are reviewed. The report concludes with recommendations intended to assist NSF and other funding agencies in the review and development of their education research portfolios. These recommendations should also prove useful to researchers and policymakers in developing criteria and guidelines for conducting rigorous scientific research on the effectiveness of educational programs and practices. These types of studies may be especially valuable for policymakers in establishing and assessing funding priorities.

This report is not intended to be a definitive guide for researchers interested in conducting studies based on experimental and observational data. Its purpose is to explain the value of quasi-experimental techniques that can be used to approximate randomized experiments. The report does not address many of the nuances of experimental and quasi-experimental designs. The goal is to describe the logic of causal inference for researchers and policymakers who are not necessarily trained in experimental and quasi-experimental designs and statistical techniques.

Chapter 1 Notes

4   There are other examples of increased interest in the use of multiple methods for making causal inferences. Groups such as the American Psychological Association, AERA, and federal agencies such as NSF have held meetings within the last few years to address how multiple methods can inform causal inference. Also see Raudenbush (2005) on multimethod research and causal analysis.

5   See Schneider, McDonald, Brown, Schalliol, Makela, Yamaguchi, et al. (2006), for a summary of varying perspectives on *Scientific Research in Education* by authors who cited the report.

2. Causality: Forming an Evidential Base

RESEARCH DESIGNS ARE DEFINED by the types of questions asked. In the case of randomized controlled experiments, the question is: What is the effect of a specific program or intervention? An intervention, such as a curricular innovation, can be viewed as the cause of an effect, such as improved student learning. "A *cause* is that which makes any other thing, either simple idea, substance, or mode, begin to be; and an *effect* is that which had its beginning from some other thing" (Locke, 1690/1975, p. 325). As Shadish, Cook, and Campbell (2002) observe, however, we rarely know all of the causes of observed effects or how they relate to one another. Holland (1986) points out that a true cause cannot be determined unequivocally; rather, we seek the probability that an effect will occur. Estimating the likelihood that an effect will occur allows the researcher the opportunity to explore why certain effects occur in some situations but not in others. For example, a given tutorial technique may be shown to help some students perform better on an achievement test; however, when this technique is used with a different population, by a different teacher, it may not be as effective. When estimating an effect, the analyst is not measuring the true relationship between a cause and an effect, but the likelihood that the cause created the effect.

The Logic of Causal Inference

In an analysis of causal effects, it is helpful to distinguish between the inference model used to specify the relationship between a cause and an effect and the statistical procedures used to determine the strength of that relationship. Hedges (2006) notes that "the inference model . . . specifies precisely the parameters we wish to estimate or test. . . . This is conceptually distinct from the *statistical analysis procedure*, which defines the mathematical procedure that will be used to test hypotheses about the treatment effect" (p. 3). For example, a researcher may be interested in determining whether a new curricular program is more effective than an existing program in increasing student learning outcomes. In this case, the effect to be estimated is how much better, on average, a population of students might do with the program than without the program. The goal of the analysis is to draw a causal inference or conclusion about the effect of the new program, relative to the existing program, on some outcome of interest. Once an inference model is specified, a set of statistical procedures can be used to test a hypothesis about the treatment effect (e.g., that the students in the new program score significantly higher on some measure of learning than students in the existing program).

The focus in the example above is on identifying the effect of a cause rather than the cause of an effect. This is the approach taken by Donald Rubin and his colleagues in statistics (see, e.g., Holland, 1986, 1988; Holland & Rubin, 1983; Imbens & Rubin, 1997; Rubin, 1974, 1978, 1980), and it has the advantage of being able to specify the cause and effect in question. For example, if a researcher is interested in knowing whether an innovative year-long mathematics program is more effective in increasing the mathematics achievement of first graders than a conventional mathematics program, then an experiment can be designed in which the effects of the two mathematics programs are compared using some appropriate post-treatment measure of mathematics achievement. If children in the innovative mathematics program score higher, on average, on the mathematics assessment than do those in the conventional program, and if the students in the two groups are equivalent in all respects other than program assignment, the researcher can conclude that the higher mathematics scores are the result of the innovative mathematics program rather than of initial differences in mathematics ability. When correctly implemented, the randomized controlled experiment is the most powerful design for detecting treatment effects. The random assignment of participants to treatment conditions assures that treatment group assignment is independent of the pretreatment characteristics of group members; thus differences between groups can be attributed to treatment effects rather than to the pretreatment characteristics. Randomized experiments, however, indicate only whether there are treatment effects and the magnitude of those effects; they do not identify the mechanisms (i.e., the specific aspects of the treatments in question or of the settings in which they are implemented) that may be contributing to such effects.[6]

Designs are not developed in a vacuum; they are guided by questions that are derived from both theory and prior research. Research questions suggest boundaries for developing or selecting appropriate methods of investigation. When treatment groups can be clearly identified and there is reason to believe that one treatment may be more effective than another, an experimental approach is warranted for detecting treatment effects. Although randomized controlled experiments are designed to detect average differences in the effects of different treatments on outcomes of interest such as student achievement, researchers need to recognize that there are a series of steps that precede the design and fielding of an experiment. In the example above, the first and most important step is to specify a theory about how students learn and what conditions contribute to student learning outcomes.

There are instances where experiments are not warranted, however. For example, if we had valid evidence in favor of a new treatment, it would be unethical to administer the old treatment.[7] In other cases we may not have sufficient evidence to suggest that one treatment is more effective than another. In these instances, exploratory descriptive analyses of pedagogical techniques that are associated with student learning outcomes for certain populations may be a more appropriate first step. Even if there is evidence to suggest that an existing program is more effective than another, it may not be logistically, financially, or ethically feasible to conduct an experiment to test this assumption. In such instances it is sometimes possible to use large-scale datasets to approximate a randomized experiment using statistical techniques. Such quasi-experiments can be used to draw causal inferences about treatment effects based on observational data.[8]

There is a long tradition in public health that builds the case for using exploratory descriptive analyses somewhat differently, and this tradition has value for the social and education sciences as well (see Kellam & Langevin, 2003). For example, hypotheses can be generated by analyses of both cross-sectional and longitudinal data. Theory is then brought in to refine the hypotheses, which are then tested in small-scale experiments, often under highly controlled situations (i.e., high internal validity, termed *efficacy trials*). If one or more efficacy trials suggest the viability of the hypothesis, then the experiment is conducted under more "real world" conditions, in what are termed effectiveness trials. These are the clinical trials that we are familiar with.[9] What this example shows is that there is also a place for non-experimental methods in the development of experiments.

The Formal Specification of the Causal Inference Model

Ideally, we would like to know what would have happened if an individual exposed to one treatment condition had instead been exposed to a different treatment condition. In practice this is not possible; for example, a student who completes one mathematics program cannot go back in time and complete a different program so that we can compare the two outcomes. However, Rubin and his colleagues use this hypothetical situation as the starting point for their conceptualization of causal effects.[10] Rubin (1974, 1977, 1978, 1980) defined a causal effect as the difference between what would have happened to the participant in the treatment condition and what would have happened to the same participant if he or she had instead been exposed to the control condition. This conceptualization is often referred to as the counterfactual account of causality. This hypothetical causal effect is defined as

$$\delta_u = Y_{t_u} - Y_{c_u},$$

where δ_u is the difference in the effects of the conditions on unit (person) **u**, **t** refers to the treatment condition, **c** refers to the control condition, and **Y** is the observed response outcome. While this definition provides a clear theoretical formulation of what a causal effect is, it cannot be tested empirically because if we have observed Y_{t_u} we cannot also observe Y_{c_u}. This is often referred to as the fundamental problem of causal inference.

Expanding on Rubin's formulation, Holland (1986) identifies two general approaches to solving this problem, which he refers to as the *scientific solution* and the *statistical solution*. The scientific solution makes certain assumptions about the objects or units of study which are often reasonable when those objects are physical entities. In one application of the scientific solution, an object or objects are first exposed to treatment 1 and the outcome of interest is measured; the object is then exposed to treatment 2 and the outcome is measured. The causal effect in this case is defined as the difference between the outcome that unit **u** displayed at time 1 under the treatment condition and the outcome that same unit displayed at time 2 under the control condition: $\delta_u = Y_{t1}(u) - Y_{c2}(u)$. Two assumptions are made in this case. The first is *temporal stability*, which means that there is a constancy of response over time. The second is *causal transience*, which means that the effect of the first treatment is transient and does not affect the object's response to the second treatment.

A second way of applying the scientific solution is to assume that the objects under study are identical in all respects. It therefore makes no difference which unit receives the treatment. This is the assumption of *unit homogeneity*. Under this assumption, the causal effect can be determined by calculating the difference between $Y_t(u_1)$ and $Y_c(u_2)$, where $Y_t(u_1)$ is the outcome of unit 1 under the treatment condition and $Y_c(u_2)$ is the outcome of unit 2 under the control condition. The assumption of unit homogeneity is often made in the physical sciences and engineering, where the objects of study have a high degree of uniformity.

When human beings are the focus of study, these assumptions are usually much less plausible. For example, a participant's response to a treatment may vary according to the time at which the treatment is delivered, invalidating the assumption of temporal stability. Similarly, a participant's response to one treatment condition may affect his or her response to a second treatment condition, invalidating the assumption of causal transience. Even if participants in an experiment are identical twins and are known to have identical genes, they may differ in other ways that may affect their responses (e.g., knowledge, experience, motivation); the assumption of unit homogeneity is rarely plausible when the unit of analysis is the person.

The statistical solution to the fundamental problem of causal inference takes a different approach. Rather than focusing on specific units, the statistical approach estimates an *average* causal effect for a population of units (i.e., participants). The population average causal effect thus becomes

$$\delta = E(Y_t - Y_c),$$

where Y_t is the average outcome for participants in the treatment group, and Y_c is the average outcome for participants in the control group.[11] For this solution to work, however, individuals or organizational elements (e.g., classrooms or schools) in the treatment and control groups should differ only in terms of treatment group assignment, not on any other characteristic or prior experience that might potentially affect their responses. For example, if the outcome of interest is mathematics achievement, and only high-achieving students are assigned to the treatment condition (e.g., an innovative mathematics program) while low-achieving students are assigned to the control condition (a conventional mathematics program), higher average mathematics scores for students in the treatment group could be due to the higher initial achievement of these students rather than to the program of instruction. However, if students are randomly assigned to the treatment and control conditions, one could expect that treatment group assignment would, *on average*, over repeated trials, be independent of any measured or unmeasured pretreatment characteristic. Because random assignment assures, in expectation, equivalence between groups on pretreatment characteristics, if students in the treatment group score higher on a post-treatment assessment of mathematics achievement, the researcher can conclude, at least in large samples, that this effect is due to differences in the program of instruction rather than to differences in the characteristics of students in the two groups.

This example represents the ideal case and assumes that the innovative program is implemented with fidelity, that students do not move between treatment and control groups, and that they remain in their assigned groups for the longevity of the study. In practice, problems in implementing experiments can present substantial threats to their validity and need to be addressed. Some of these problems and proposed solutions to them are discussed in the next section.

The statistical solution to the fundamental problem of causality relies on the assumption of independence between pretreatment characteristics and treatment group assignment. This independence is difficult to achieve in nonrandomized studies. Statistical models typically are used to adjust for potentially confounding variables (i.e., characteristics of students, classrooms, or schools that predict treatment group assignment and also predict outcomes) when outcomes for different groups are compared. However, as Raudenbush (2005) points out, "No matter how many potential confounders [analysts] identify and control, the burden of proof is always on the [analysts] to argue that no important confounders have been omitted" (p. 28). Because randomized assignment to treatment groups takes into account observed and unobserved characteristics, such controls are not necessary. This is why randomized field trials are often considered the "gold standard" for making causal inferences.

Criteria for Making Causal Inferences

In elaborating on Rubin's causal model, Holland (1986) identifies four criteria for making causal inferences. He relies on examples from controlled experiments to illustrate these criteria. "It is not that an experiment is the *only* proper setting for discovering causality," he writes, "but I do feel that an experiment is the *simplest* such setting" (p. 946).

Causal Relativity

The effect of a cause must always be evaluated relative to another cause. In a controlled experiment, for example, the outcomes for a given treatment or intervention (one cause) are always defined relative to an alternative treatment or control condition (a second cause). Thus, in evaluating whether an innovative mathematics program is effective in increasing mathematics achievement, the outcomes of the program must be compared with the outcomes from some existing program. The question is not simply whether a program is effective but whether it is more effective than some other program.

Causal Manipulation

Each participant must be *potentially* exposable to the causes under consideration (i.e., the treatment and control conditions). For example, the instruction a student receives can be said to be a cause of the student's performance on a test, in the sense used by Holland, whereas the student's race or gender may not. Race and gender are attributes of the student that cannot typically be altered or manipulated and thus cannot be said to be causes of differences in mathematics achievement. In contrast, a student can potentially be exposed to different types of instruction.

Temporal Ordering

Exposure to a cause must occur at a specific time or within a specific time period. In determining whether students who participate in an innovative mathematics program earn higher scores on a mathematics assessment than those who participate in an existing mathematics program, the researcher must obtain students' mathematics scores after their exposure to either the treatment or control condition. In this instance, the outcome variable (post-exposure mathematics scores) serves as a measure of the effect of the treatment. Variables thus divide into two classes: pre-exposure—those whose values are determined prior to exposure to the cause (the treatment or control condition)—and post-exposure—those whose values are determined after exposure to the cause.

Elimination of Alternative Explanations

The researcher must be able to rule out alternative explanations for the relationship between a possible cause or treatment and an effect (as measured by an outcome of interest). In controlled experiments, this is accomplished in part through the random assignment of participants to treatment and control groups. Although there may be difficulties in implementing randomization (an issue addressed later), in the ideal situation, when randomization is effective, treatment and control groups are essentially equivalent with respect to pretreatment characteristics. Any differences in the outcomes of the two groups can thus be attributed to differences in treatment assignment rather than to other causes such as pretreatment differences in ability, achievement, learning experiences, or other characteristics.

Issues in the Design and Fielding of Randomized Experiments

Sampling Imbalances

Complete equivalence on all pretreatment characteristics is rarely achieved even when random assignment is used. As Raudenbush (2005) notes, random assignment does not necessarily ensure that there will be no differences between treatment and control groups: "It is true, by chance, differences will exist among randomly formed groups; and these differences may in fact, be quite large in small samples. But such chance differences are fully accounted for by well-known and comparatively simple methods of statistical inference" (p. 27). Typically, however, researchers compare treatment and control groups on key variables (e.g., demographics such as gender, race, socioeconomic status [SES], and so on) to make sure that randomization has been effective (see, e.g., Krueger, 1999; Nye, Konstantopoulos, & Hedges, 2000). Another way in which this issue is addressed is through replication of studies and cross-study comparisons. The comparison of results across randomized controlled experiments allows researchers to obtain more accurate estimates of causal effects and it increases the confidence that the result is real, not due to sampling fluctuations.

Specific Versus Average Effects

Because the statistical solution to the fundamental problem of causal inference estimates an average effect for a population of participants or units, it tells us nothing about the causal effect for specific participants or subgroups of participants. Holland (1986) observes that this average effect "may be of interest for its own sake in certain types of studies. It would be of interest to a state education director who wanted to know what reading program would be the best to give to all of the first graders in his state. The average causal effect of the best program would be reflected in increases in statewide average reading scores" (p. 949). But, in other cases, researchers might be interested in knowing whether certain programs would help to close achievement gaps between particular groups of students.[12] In such cases, researchers would be less interested in knowing whether the treatment produces a constant effect (one relevant to every participant in the study) and more interested in knowing whether treatment effects vary across subgroups of students. Holland notes that the assumption of a constant effect can be checked by dividing the sample into subpopulations; an average causal effect can then be estimated for each subgroup.

Atypical Responses

Rubin (1986) observes that two additional assumptions must be valid for randomization to yield unbiased estimates of causal effects. These are ideal criteria that are frequently not met in educational and other social science research.[13] However, they are important because they help to guide researchers in the design of their studies.

First, the mechanism for assigning participants to treatment and control groups should not affect their responses. In many studies this assumption may not be valid. For example, if disadvantaged high school students are told that they have been chosen at random to participate in a program designed to encourage college attendance, they may respond differently than if they are told that they were selected on the basis of their academic achievement. Those who believe they were selected on the basis of merit may be more motivated to participate in the program and more likely to apply to college. If the goal is to determine whether the program is effective in increasing college-going rates for disadvantaged students, then students' knowledge of the assignment mechanism may affect the outcome of interest.

Second, the responses of participants should not be affected by the treatment received by other participants. For example, if participants in the control group know that those in the treatment group are participating in a promising new program, they may become demoralized because they are not receiving the program. Alternatively, they may respond competitively and do better than they might have otherwise. Estimates of treatment effects would be biased upward in the first instance and downward in the second.

Researchers have developed several strategies for minimizing atypical responses. If participants are only aware of the condition in which they participate, their responses to the treatment or control condition will be unaffected by the use of random assignment. In practice, however, this solution may not be feasible, particularly if informed consent procedures require that participants be told that they will be randomly assigned to different treatment conditions. Another strategy for minimizing atypical responses is the use of masking or blinding procedures: Participants are not told whether they have been assigned to the treatment or control group. The experimenter is also, in many cases, unaware of which group participants are assigned to, a procedure known as double-blinding. In triple-blinding, not even the data analyst knows which participants were assigned to the treatment and control conditions. However, masking procedures often are not feasible in real-world situations, where participants may need to know that they are receiving a particular treatment or benefit for the experiment to work (e.g., financial assistance). In other cases, participants may be able to identify their treatment group assignment despite masking procedures. A third strategy that is sometimes used in randomized studies is to offer participants in the control group a program that is equally as attractive as the treatment condition but has no relation to the response of interest.[14]

Implementing Randomized Assignment

Implementing experiments with randomized assignment can also present problems for researchers, such as breakdowns in randomization, treatment noncompliance, and attrition.[15] Researchers who use randomized designs are familiar with these potential problems, and considerable strides have been made to overcome them (see Shadish, Cook, & Campbell, 2002). The value of conducting experiments in education and an assessment of the objections to doing them are discussed by Cook (2002, 2007).

Problems in conducting experiments are also common in other types of research such as large-scale surveys. For example, when random sample of schools are drawn, some schools may choose not to participate, some may drop out during data collection, and some may fail to comply with survey procedures and administration. Methodologists have developed a number of procedures for addressing such problems, although such solutions are not always adequate. Next, we review some of these problems and ways in which they have been addressed in randomized field trials.

Breakdowns in randomization. There is sometimes resistance to randomization, particularly when a promising new treatment is being tested. For example, parents may lobby to have their children included in a promising new program. Such problems can be avoided by monitoring both the randomization process and the actual treatment received by each participant following randomization. Another strategy to minimize breakdowns in randomization is to isolate the units under study. For example, when different treatments are given to different schools (high isolation of units), it is less likely that breakdowns in randomization will occur than when different treatments are given to different classrooms within the same school (low isolation of units).[16]

Treatment noncompliance. Individuals who are randomly assigned to treatment and control conditions may never actually receive treatment. Some may simply fail to show up for the particular program to which they have been assigned. For example, randomly assigning students (families) to receive a Catholic school voucher does not mean that they will use the voucher (e.g., because of family beliefs about public education, proximity to alternative schools, or other reasons). There are several practical ways to encourage participation, such as providing incentives, removing obstacles (e.g., providing transportation), and including only those who are willing to participate. Even when such steps are taken, however, some of those selected for participation in a study may still fail to participate.

Three statistical strategies have been used in cases where there is participant noncompliance. In the first approach, known as the *intention to treat analysis,* the mean responses of those assigned to the treatment condition (regardless of whether they actually received treatment) are compared with the mean responses of those assigned to the control condition. Since noncompliers do not receive treatment, the mean for the treatment group is typically lower than it would be if all individuals assigned to the treatment condition had actually received treatment, assuming that the treatment has positive effects. As a result, this analysis usually yields conservative estimates of treatment effects. The second approach eliminates individuals assigned to the treatment condition who do not actually receive the treatment. Unless it can be shown that those who drop out of the treatment condition are a random sample of the participants in that condition, this analysis will yield a biased estimate of the treatment effect.

The third strategy focuses on estimating the intention to treat effect for the subset of participants who are "true compliers." True compliers are those who will take the treatment when assigned it and will take the control when assigned it. Noncompliers are those who will not take what they are assigned, whether it is the treatment or the control condition (Angrist, Imbens, & Rubin, 1996; Bloom, 1984; Little & Yau, 1998). Noncompliers are of three possible types: never-takers, who will never take treatment no matter what condition they are assigned to; always-takers, who will always take treatment no matter what condition they are assigned to; and defiers, who will always do the opposite of what they are assigned (these people are often assumed not to exist or to be few in number).

Because only the true compliers can be observed both taking and not taking treatment, they are the only subgroup for which we can learn about the effect of taking treatment versus being in the control group.

An additional assumption yields the *instrumental variable estimate* for the noncompliers: There is no effect of the assignment on what would be observed.[17] That is, the "exclusion restriction" says that if the assignment to treatment versus control cannot affect which condition a participant will take (i.e., the noncompliers will do what they want regardless of the condition to which they are assigned), it cannot affect the participants' outcome. Extensions of this approach that weaken various assumptions and deal with complications, such as missing data, also exist (e.g., Imbens & Rubin, 1997; Rubin, 1998; Frangakis & Rubin, 1999; Hirano, Imbens, Rider, & Rubin, 2001).

Attrition. In many cases, individuals selected for study initially participate but later drop out. It is not always possible to maintain contact with all participants, and those who are contacted may refuse to continue their participation. Researchers have been aware of this issue for some time (see, e.g., Jurs & Glass, 1971) and have developed strategies for estimating the effect of attrition on the outcomes of interest.

Little and Rubin (2002) review several techniques for dealing with missing data, including data missing due to attrition. They also identify mechanisms that lead to missing data. Identifying such mechanisms is important in selecting an appropriate method for handling missing data. Little and Rubin identify three categories of missing-data mechanisms: missing completely at random, missing at random, and not missing at random. Data are said to missing completely at random (MCAR) if the probability of having missing data on an outcome variable Y is not dependent on Y or on any of the variables included in analysis. If data are missing completely at random, estimates of treatment outcomes are unbiased. Data are said to be missing at random (MAR) if the likelihood of having missing data is related to the observed values of other variables included in the analysis. In this case, the missing data are unrelated to **Y** after controlling for other variables. For example, individuals who drop out of a study may have lower incomes than those who remain in the study. However, if this pattern is accounted for by relationships among observed variables, such as race and education, then data are missing at random, and estimates of treatment effects are unbiased. In cases where data are not missing at random (NMAR), the probability of having missing data is dependent on both observed and unobserved values of the outcome **Y**. For example, attrition may depend on values that were recorded after dropout. If only individuals with incomes below a certain level drop out of the study, and data on income are available only for those who remain in the study, then estimates of treatment effects will be biased.

As Foster and Fang (2004) note in their review of methods for handling attrition, "In any given situation, the actual missing data mechanism is unknown. However, . . . the evaluator can assess the plausibility of the alternative assumptions based on what he or she knows about the evaluation and the population included and what they reveal about how the missing data were generated" (p. 438). In cases of attrition from randomized experiments, researchers typically have information on the pretreatment characteristics of participants as well as their treatment group assignments and can conduct analyses to determine whether there are any significant differences on pretest measures between those who drop out of the study and those who remain in the study. Significant differences between leavers and stayers indicate that the characteristics of those who leave the study differ from the characteristics of those who remain in the study, suggesting that the study findings may not generalize to the population of interest.

When the characteristics of participants who drop out of the treatment group differ from the characteristics of those who drop out of the control group, the estimate of the treatment effect may be biased. In such cases, researchers should cautiously explore techniques for adjusting for potential bias (e.g., imputing missing values, modeling the effects of attrition on responses, and estimating maximum and minimum values to bracket the treatment effect).[18]

Detecting Treatment Effects

Statistical power. In the context of experimentation, *power* refers to the ability of a statistical test to detect a true treatment effect, that is, to detect a treatment effect when it in fact exists. Existing reviews of the literature indicate that insufficient power for making statistical judgments is a problem with studies in several fields, including medicine (see, e.g., Cuijpers, 2003; Dignam, 2003; Halpern, Karlawish, & Berlin, 2002; Rossi, 1990; West, Biesanz, & Pitts, 2000). This is a serious problem, given both the cost of conducting randomized experiments and the failure of underpowered studies to yield consistent answers. As Dignam argues with respect to randomized clinical trials:

> It is imperative that [randomized experiments] be carefully designed with respect to statistical power so as not to obtain equivocal findings that fail to answer the fundamental question of a new treatment under consideration. Underpowered studies can cause delay or even abandonment of promising avenues of treatment, and even a "negative" that is adequately powered is an important finding in that energy and resources can be directed into other more promising alternatives (p. 6).

There are several methods for increasing statistical power. Increasing sample size is the most obvious, but practical considerations such as cost, available resources, and access to populations of interest (e.g., children with learning disabilities) may restrict this option for researchers. Other approaches to increasing statistical power include using more reliable measures, minimizing participant attrition, increasing the fidelity of treatment implementation, and measuring and adjusting for characteristics related to the outcome of interest.[19]

Hedges (2006) observes that increasing the significance level (denoted by α) used in statistical testing is one way to increase power without increasing sample size. He notes that "statistical decision theory recognizes two kinds of errors that can be made in testing. The significance level controls the rate of Type I Errors (rejecting the null hypothesis when it is true). Setting a low significance level [such as the conventional $\alpha = .05$] to control Type I Errors [concluding there are treatment effects when there are in fact no effects] actually increases the rate of Type II Errors (failing to detect effects that are actually present)" (p. 20). He argues that when resources are limited, as is the case in many intervention studies, "selection of a significance level other than .05 (such as .10 or even .20) may be reasonable choices to balance considerations of power and protection against Type I Errors" (p. 20).

The use of stratified randomization can also increase power. In small-scale randomized studies, treatment and control groups may not be well matched on certain characteristics such as age or gender. In such cases, the use of stratified randomization can increase the balance between treatment and control groups without sacrificing the advantages of randomization. Stratified randomization is achieved by performing separate randomizations with each subset of participants (e.g., as defined by gender, age, and pretreatment assessment scores).

Software packages now available for making power calculations allow researchers to compute the sample size needed to detect a treatment effect of a given size in advance of conducting an experiment. Often, an estimate of the effect size for a particular treatment/intervention is available from prior research, especially meta-analyses. Following Cohen (1988), many researchers also rely on general "rules of thumb" about what constitutes large, medium, and small effect sizes. Tools for computing statistical power for multilevel studies (e.g., students nested within schools) are less widely available, but there have been some advances in this area (McDonald, Keesler, Kauffman, & Schneider, 2006). Researchers have found that increasing sample sizes at higher levels (e.g., schools or sites) increases power more effectively than increasing sample sizes at lower levels (e.g., students within schools; Raudenbush & Liu, 2000). Adding another site to a study, however, may be considerably more costly than adding participants within a site.

One problem faced by education researchers has been a lack of definitive knowledge about school-level characteristics associated with academic achievement. To address this problem, Hedges and his colleagues, with support from the IERI, have begun to identify factors contributing to within- and between-school variation in academic achievement. Reanalyzing data from surveys administered to nationally representative samples of students, they are conducting analyses of variation in mathematics and reading achievement "separately (by subject matter) for different grade levels, regions of the country and urbanicity (coded as urban, suburban, or rural)" (Hedberg, Santana, & Hedges, 2004, p. 5). They have found that academic achievement varies significantly at the school as well as the individual level; achievement also varies significantly by region of the country, urbanicity, and students' stage in the life-course. These findings, which the authors plan to compile into an almanac, should be useful to researchers in designing adequately powered studies.

Generalizability in experimental studies. Experiments provide the best evidence with respect to treatment effects;

student achievement. Smaller-scale studies that assess aspects of students' conceptual understanding, content knowledge, and procedural knowledge in different subject areas are also important in identifying gaps in student proficiency. Without such studies, researchers and policymakers would not know what outcomes most need to be improved and for which students. Raudenbush argues that

> a failure to attend systematically to this process of creating good outcome measures [may be] the Achilles heel of evaluation research on instructional innovation. If the process is ignored, trivialized, or mismanaged, we'll be measuring the wrong outcome with high reliability, the right outcome with low reliability, or, in the worst case, we won't know what we are measuring. If we don't know what we are measuring, the causal question (Does the new intervention improve achievement?) is meaningless. If we measure the right outcome unreliably, we will likely find a new program ineffective even if it is effective. If we measure the wrong outcome reliably, we may find that the intervention "works," but we'll never know whether it works to achieve our goals. (2005, p. 29).

Identifying promising interventions. Studies that identify interventions that are promising candidates for large-scale randomized trials are another important component of research designed to improve student learning. Raudenbush notes that a variety of methods can be used to identify promising interventions that could be implemented on a large scale:

> Detailed descriptions of expert practice often supply key new ideas for how to intervene. Small-scale implementation studies or even careful small-scale randomized studies can provide preliminary evidence about whether a new approach can, under ideal conditions, produce an effect for a sample that probably is not representative. Secondary analysis of large-scale data can provide important evidence of promising practice. (2005, p. 29)

Targeting populations of interest. In designing large-scale randomized experiments, information is also needed on the populations of students who are in the greatest need of educational interventions or would benefit most from new approaches to teaching and learning. A variety of methods have been used to determine where achievement gaps exist and for what populations of students, as well as what settings, organizational approaches, and instructional methods might help to reduce such gaps.

Fielding Randomized Experiments in Educational Settings

To assist the education research community in conducting randomized controlled trials, the NRC (2004b) sponsored a workshop and issued a report on the practical problems of conducting such studies. This report discusses a number of pragmatic issues that must be addressed in conducting randomized controlled trials (RCTs) in educational settings: meeting ethical and legal standards, establishing adequate sample sizes and recruiting participants, grounding the study in the relevant educational context, and securing adequate resources.[20] Each of these issues is important to the success of RCTs in obtaining valid evidence of treatment effects.

Researchers, including those conducting randomized controlled trials, are now required to meet rigorous legal and ethical standards for conducting research with human subjects. For example, in implementing a randomized controlled experiment with students, researchers must inform parents of the goals and nature of the research and obtain their consent for their children's participation. The researchers also must demonstrate that procedures are in place to ensure that individual information and identifying data are confidential. In some cases, researchers may have trouble obtaining approval from institutional review boards (IRBs) responsible for ensuring that studies meet legal and ethical standards, particularly if an intervention has the potential to harm participants (e.g., an intervention involving a vigorous exercise program).

Despite such safeguards, many potential participants have ethical concerns about RCTs that have received IRB approval, particularly when randomized assignment is perceived as denying beneficial services or interventions to some students. Researchers need to be aware of and address such concerns both in designing and in implementing RCTs. One way in which researchers have dealt with this issue at the school level is to include participating schools in both the treatment and control conditions. For example, in designing and implementing Success for All, Slavin and his colleagues randomly assigned schools to treatment and control conditions (see, e.g., Slavin & Madden, 2001, in press; Slavin, Madden, Karweit, Dolan, & Wasik, 1992; Slavin, Madden, Dolan, Wasik, Ross, & Smith, 1994). However, the intervention was implemented in first grade in one set of schools, with first graders in the other schools serving as the control group. In schools that had served as the first grade control group, the intervention was implemented in third grade, with the first grade intervention group serving as the control. Schools in both groups thus had the opportunity to participate in an intervention that might prove beneficial to students. As Slavin and others have noted, developing close and respectful partnerships with schools and school districts is an effective way to become aware of and address such concerns.

Ensuring that samples are sufficiently large to detect effects can be particularly difficult in certain educational settings. For example, in urban settings, high rates of mobility can make it difficult for researchers to recruit and retain sufficient numbers of study participants. Obtaining consent from parents may also prove to be difficult. Given enough time, researchers can meet with parents to inform them about the study and address their concerns. Building partnerships with schools can facilitate the process of recruitment, but establishing such partnerships can be a lengthy process, requiring that relationships be established years in advance of the implementation of a randomized controlled trial.

Grounding a study in the relevant educational setting (e.g., addressing questions of particular interest to participating schools and teachers) can help to build partnerships with schools that support the implementation of randomized experiments. Determining what questions are most pressing for particular schools and teachers requires a familiarity with the political and economic environment of schools, the schools' missions and goals, and the particular challenges they face. For example, in designing interventions to reduce drug abuse, delinquency, and school failure, Kellam and his colleagues (Kellam & Van Horn, 1997; Kellam, Ling, Merisca, Brown, & Ialongo, 1998) targeted Baltimore schools that were struggling to find solutions to these problems. This partnership with the Baltimore school system has made it possible for Kellam and his colleagues to conduct three generations of randomized controlled trials.

Questions about whether a widely used educational intervention has systematic effects on student learning outcomes are often best answered by large-scale randomized field trials. However, such studies can be costly to implement, particularly when treatments are assigned at the school level, requiring the inclusion of a sufficient number of schools to detect treatment effects. When trying to measure changes in performance, such as gains in achievement, accurately assessing growth requires that trials be conducted over a sufficient period of time, typically at least a year, which also adds to the costs of fielding the study. Given such costs, it is particularly important that these studies be well designed, have a strong theoretical grounding, and be adequately informed by prior research. In some cases, the research base may be insufficient to justify fielding an RCT. In such cases, researchers may need to conduct preliminary descriptive studies or smaller-scale randomized studies to determine whether an intervention is sufficiently promising to warrant large-scale implementation and the development of adequate measures for the variables of interest. In other cases, RCTs may not be feasible, either because of costs or for ethical reasons, and researchers may need to approximate randomized experiments with observational data. Analyzing data from large-scale datasets can be useful in both instances by providing tentative results needed to design and implement effective large-scale randomized trials or by providing alternative methods for making valid causal inferences with observational data.

Chapter 2 Notes

6   Randomized experiments can be used in conjunction with other methods to examine the mechanisms that help explain causes.

7   In education experimental studies that involve treatment and control groups, it is nearly always the case that the "control group" means business as usual. It is rare for an experiment to withhold treatment.

8   Several of these techniques are described in Section 3.

9   We thank George Bohrnstedt for this point.

10 There is a long history of work in statistics that has focused on causal inference. Rubin's model builds on this tradition, which includes early work on experimental design by Fisher (1935), Neyman (1923, 1935), Cochran and Cox (1950), Kempthorne (1952), and Cox (1958a, 1958b).

11 Technically, **E** is the expected value or long-run average of the difference on **Y** between the treatment and control groups.

12 One advantage of descriptive studies that rely on large-scale nationally representative datasets is that it is possible to examine subgroups of participants because samples are large and representative of the population.

13 These criteria are referred to as the stable-unit-treatment-value assumption (SUTVA).

14 See, for example, Higginbotham, West, and Forsyth (1988) and West, Biesanz, and Pitts (2000) for discussions of atypical reactions and strategies for dealing with them.

15 See West et al. (2000) for a useful review of several of these problems.

16 When schools or other groups are assigned to treatment conditions, randomization occurs at the group rather than the individual level (see Raudenbush, 1997, for a discussion of cluster randomization). The assumption that individual responses are independent is not valid in this situation because individuals within the same group are more likely to provide similar responses than individuals in different groups. This problem is now routinely dealt with by using hierarchical linear modeling procedures, which simultaneously provide estimates of causal effects at both the individual and group levels, while

correcting for the nonindependence of responses within groups (Bryk & Raudenbush, 2002).

17 Instrumental variable approaches are discussed in Section 3. We thank Donald Rubin for writing the section on estimating complier average causal effects and for offering additional explanation of this technique.

18 Several different software programs are available for computing missing values: SOLAS™ for Missing Data Analysis (available at http:// www.statsol.ie/solas/solas.htm); SAS-based IVEware (available at http://www.isr.umich.edu/src/smp/ive); MICE (Multiple Imputation by Chain Equations, available at http://www.multiple-imputation. com); and NORM and related programs (available at http://www.stat. psu.edu/%7Ejls/misoftwa.html).

19 See Shadish, Cook, and Campbell (2002, pp. 46–47) for an overview of strategies for increasing power.

20 There is a common misconception that randomized experiments are always expensive. In the context of this report, we are discussing the costs of conducting large-scale, multi-site randomized experiments. Regardless of whether studies employ an experimental or a quasi-experimental approach, most national multi-site, longitudinal collections are expensive. We thank Thomas Cook for pointing this out.

3. Estimating Causal Effects Using Observational Data

SOME OF THE MOST IMPORTANT theoretical and methodological work in education research has resulted from data analyses using large-scale national datasets such as the Early Childhood Longitudinal Study (ECLS) and the National Education Longitudinal Study of 1988–2000 (NELS). For example, two award-winning books, *Public and Private High Schools: The Impact of Communities* (Coleman & Hoffer, 1987) and *Catholic Schools and the Common Good* (Bryk, Lee, & Holland, 1993), were based on analyses of High School and Beyond (HS&B), a longitudinal study of high school students in the 1980s. The number of dissertations, articles in refereed journals, and other publications that have been written from these national datasets is well over 10,000. Large-scale datasets that are drawn from multistage probability samples allow for predictive analyses and tentative causal inference. Investigators can estimate the probable effects of certain conditions for specific populations over time. In instances where there are data elements about school or pedagogical practices, analytic techniques can estimate the likelihood of what would happen if certain organizational, institutional, or instructional reforms were implemented on a larger scale.

In some cases, such datasets can also be used to approximate randomized controlled experiments. For example, matched sampling has been used to assess the causal effects of interventions when randomized experiments cannot be conducted (Rubin, 2006). Over the past three decades, statisticians (e.g., Rubin, 1974, 1978; Rosenbaum, 1986) and econometricians (e.g., Heckman, 1976, 1979) have developed several methods of analysis for making causal inferences with observational data such as large-scale national datasets.

There are several advantages to using large-scale, nationally representative datasets to study student achievement differences. Large-scale studies, such as NELS, are based on nationally representative samples of U.S. students and their parents, schools, and teachers. In contrast to randomized controlled experiments, which are designed to yield valid causal results but often have limited generalizability, large-scale national educational studies are designed to be generalizable to specific populations of students, such as high school students in the United States. Large-scale datasets thus serve as a rich source of descriptive information on students, teachers, and schools. Because they are based on large, nationally representative samples, such datasets are also useful in studying the characteristics and achievement of subgroups such as minority and low-income students, groups that are often targeted for educational interventions. In addition, such datasets are often longitudinal, making it possible for analysts to measure achievement gains at both the individual and group levels. Large-scale datasets can also be used to develop plausible hypotheses regarding the causes of differences in student achievement gains. For example, analyses of administrative data from Texas public school systems have been useful in developing some promising models for estimating teacher quality (Rivkin, Hanushek, & Kain, 2005).

Analyses of large-scale datasets can also inform the design of randomized controlled trials. Such datasets can be used to identify promising interventions, to target subgroups that are most likely to benefit from such interventions, and to suggest causal mechanisms that may explain why an innovative program may have positive effects on student achievement relative to a more conventional program. Moreover, when randomized controlled trials are not feasible, large-scale nationally representative studies may provide the best source of data on which to base educational policy decisions.

Despite their strengths, large-scale observational datasets do not typically include the random assignment of individuals or schools to treatment and control groups that is the hallmark of randomized controlled trials.[21] Researchers therefore need to be aware of the tradeoffs involved in choosing experimental versus non-experimental designs when both can be used to address a particular research question and both are financially, logistically, and ethically feasible. For example, "natural experiments" constructed from survey data are sometimes used to investigate the effects of particular educational programs or reforms (Angrist & Krueger, 2001). These methods seek to isolate comparisons that capture causal effects even without the benefit of purposeful random assignment.

When constructing treatment and control groups from observational data, researchers have limited control over the composition of the groups being compared. Those who participate in a program may differ systematically from those who do not, which can bias estimates of program effects, a problem referred to as *sample selection bias*. For example, if a researcher is trying to evaluate the effect of a high school dropout program on high school completion rates and the analysis is based only on students who complete the program, the sample used for analysis may overrepresent students at low or moderate risk of dropping out and underrepresent high-risk students who drop out of school prior to completing or entering the program (Cuddeback, Wilson, Orme, & Combs-Orme, 2004).

Researchers have developed several different procedures to adjust for selection bias. One of the earliest and most well-known techniques was developed by James Heckman (1976, 1979). In this two-step procedure, a multiple regression model is estimated for an outcome of interest (e.g., high school completion rates). A selection model is also estimated comparing those who participate in a program with those who do not participate on selected variables. If differences between participants and nonparticipants are detected, then adjustments are made to the first model to correct for these differences. There are limitations, however, to procedures used to correct for selection bias. The selection model used to detect and correct for selection differences may be misspecified. For example, important variables may be missing from the model. In such cases, attempts to correct for selection bias may actually make estimates more problematic (Stolzenberg & Relles, 1997; Winship & Mare, 1992).

In some cases, selection bias can be corrected by adjusting outcomes for relevant observables that are correlated with the outcome variable and the independent variables of interest. This has been termed *observable selection bias* (Barnow, Cain, & Goldberger, 1980). However, unobserved characteristics can also bias estimates of program effects. For example, in assessing achievement differences between public and charter school students, procedures for reducing observable selection bias may be used to adjust for differences in family characteristics such as income and structure. But there may also be unobserved characteristics that are associated with both charter school attendance and student achievement outcomes. Charter schools may attract students who are having academic difficulties in public schools. Families may enroll their children in a charter school specifically because they are already not doing as well as their public school classmates. Charter schools may also appeal to the most motivated parents, eager to provide opportunities to their children that they feel are lacking in regular private schools. In the first instance, estimates of the effect of charter schools on student achievement may be biased downward; in the second they may be biased upward. Such selection factors are often "unobservables" or omitted variables. They are correlated with the educational intervention in question and therefore bias estimates of the effect of that intervention on outcomes.[22]

Social scientists have developed several methods to adjust for observed and/or omitted variables when making comparisons across groups using observational data. These methods, which include fixed effects models, instrumental variables, propensity score matching, and regression discontinuity designs, have been used to approximate randomized controlled experiments (see Winship & Morgan, 1999, for a useful overview).[23]

Methods for Approximating Randomized Assignment

Fixed Effects Models

Many large-scale nonrandomized datasets contain multiple observations of individuals over time. Since a major concern is that unobserved characteristics are correlated with both treatment and outcome variables, controlling for such unobservables would reduce the bias in the estimate of the treatment effect. One approach to correcting for selection bias when there are identifiable treatment groups is to adjust for fixed, unobserved characteristics that may be associated with selection into the treatment group.[24] Janet Currie (2003) offers a clear example of this approach. She suggests that in looking at the effect of mother's employment on child outcomes, the mother's personality may be related to the likelihood both of being employed and of having good child outcomes. If one assumes that personality is unlikely to change over time, it can be considered a fixed characteristic. For example, women who are more "nurturing" may be more likely to stay at home with their children and to have good child outcomes. In this example, mother's employment or unemployment can be considered the treatment and control conditions; mother's personality is an unobserved characteristic that may be related both to selection into employment and child outcomes. Excluding this variable from analytic models may therefore bias estimates of the effect of mother's employment on child outcomes (e.g., maternal employment may appear to have a more negative effect on child outcomes than it actually does). Currie notes that in cases where the mother works during the infancy of one child but stays at home during the infancy of another, it is possible to compare the effects of mother's employment status on the outcomes for siblings. Because the children have the same mother, the effect of the mother's personality is assumed to be fixed, though unmeasured. The argument is that by comparing the differences in the outcomes of siblings in the two groups, the analyst can obtain an unbiased estimate of the effects of maternal employment on those outcomes.

Currie and Thomas (1995) use a similar approach in analyzing the effects of Head Start on child outcomes. Results of previous studies had consistently shown a negative relationship between Head Start attendance and student learning outcomes. However, the children served by Head Start are typically from low-income families and have parents with low levels of educational attainment. Compared with children from more advantaged families, these children consistently score lower on measures of cognitive growth. To control for differences in the background characteristics of children selected into Head Start versus those not enrolled in a Head Start program, Currie and Thomas looked at the outcomes of siblings who differed with respect to Head Start enrollment. One sibling had attended Head Start and the other had not; in most other respects, however, the children had similar background characteristics. In this instance, household effects were considered fixed since the siblings were from the same household. Using this fixed effects model, Currie and Thomas found that siblings who attended Head Start did systematically better than siblings who did not, even though children in Head Start programs had lower-than-average achievement overall. Currie and Thomas were thus able to argue that Head Start does have significant effects on child outcomes.

A study by Bifulco and Ladd (2006) provides another example of the use of fixed effects to adjust for possible bias from unobserved characteristics. The investigators analyzed a large longitudinal sample of North Carolina students that included five third-grade cohorts.[25] In addition to end-of-grade reading and mathematics test scores and data on student background characteristics, the dataset included information on whether the school was a charter or regular public school and a school identifier. Bifulco and Ladd were able to track individual students over time and identify whether they were attending a charter or regular public school in any given year. Approximately 65% of students in the sample had attended both a public school and a charter school; the investigators were thus able to compare the test score gains of students while in charter schools with the test score gains *of these same students* while in traditional public schools. Because the same students were observed in each school setting, the effects of time-invariant student characteristics (both observed and unobserved) were the same across school settings (i.e., they were "fixed" across settings; such fixed effects included the student's gender, race, and ethnicity). The strength of this method is that it does not rely on comparing charter school students to some other group of students; it therefore substantially reduces the problem of self-selection bias.[26] In comparing the outcomes of students in each setting, Bifulco and Ladd found that students in charter schools scored significantly lower in both reading and mathematics.[27]

As Currie (2003) notes, there are a number of drawbacks to using fixed effects models to correct for selection bias. First, the assumption that the unobserved characteristic is fixed or time invariant may not be valid. Mother's personality, for example, may actually change over time; or siblings may respond to their mother differently, which may potentially affect the outcome of interest. The analyst thus needs to provide a convincing rationale for why the variable should be considered fixed. Second, fixed effects models may considerably reduce the size of the sample being analyzed, making it difficult to detect treatment effects. In the case of the Head Start study, for example, only children enrolled in Head Start who had a non-enrolled sibling are used to identify the effects of Head Start. Third, the analytic sample may not be representative of the population of interest. For example, in looking at the effects of mother's employment on child outcomes, it would be helpful to know if mothers who changed their employment status between the birth of one child and the next did so for a specific reason. Mothers who worked during the infancy of one child but not another may have stayed home because the second child had health or developmental problems. Consequently, the sample analyzed would not be representative of the larger population of mothers who chose not to work. Fourth, fixed effects estimates tend to be biased in the direction of "no effect." As Currie notes, "Intuitively, we can divide a measured variable into a true 'signal' and a random 'noise' component. The true signal may be very persistent between siblings (e.g., if both children have high IQ), while the noise component may be more random (e.g., one child has a bad day on the day of the test). Hence when we look at the difference between siblings, we can end up differencing out much of the true signal (since it is similar for both siblings) and being left only with the noise" (pp. 5–6). However, when the analyst can provide a convincing rationale for regarding the variable as fixed and is working with a large dataset, fixed effects models can be a powerful means for detecting treatment effects.

Instrumental Variables

A second method to correct for omitted variables is to include an "instrumental variable" in the analysis (Angrist, Imbens, & Rubin, 1996; Angrist & Krueger, 2001). An analytic tool used primarily by economists, instrumental variables were first used over 40 years ago, to estimate supply and demand curves and then to counteract bias from measurement error (Angrist & Krueger). This approach has also been used to overcome omitted variable problems in estimating causal relationships, typically problems that are narrowly defined in scope. In estimating the effect of years of schooling on earnings, for example, the observed relationship between earnings and the explanatory variable, years of schooling, is likely to be misleading because it partially reflects omitted factors that are related to both variables, such as cognitive ability. If ability could be accurately measured and held constant in a statistical procedure like regression, then the problem of omitting this variable could be avoided. But researchers typically are unsure what the best controls are for ability, and without more detailed information, we cannot assume the contribution of ability from the relationship between schooling and earnings.

This is where the instrumental variable enters in. A good instrumental variable should be associated with the treatment or endogenous variable (years of schooling) but be uncorrelated with the omitted variable (e.g., ability) and thus have no association with the exogenous or outcome variable (earnings), except through schooling. Because the instrumental variable is correlated with years of schooling but is uncorrelated with other determinants of earnings, such as ability, the causal effect of the instrument on earnings is proportional to the causal effect of schooling on earnings.[28] Instrumental variable estimates can be computed using two-stage least squares (2SLS) regression analysis. In the first stage, the instrumental variable and any covariates are used to predict the endogenous variable (years of schooling or "treatment" in our example) in a regression equation. In the second stage, the dependent variable is regressed on fitted values from the first stage regression plus any covariates.[29] If the instrumental variable is uncorrelated with the omitted variable (ability), the predicted value of years of schooling is also uncorrelated with the omitted variable. The bias in the estimation of earnings resulting from the exclusion of ability from the model is thus removed.

In an investigation of the effect of years of schooling on earnings, Angrist and Krueger (1991) used birth date and compulsory school laws as instrumental variables, with ability, family background, and any other unobserved determinants of earnings as the omitted variables. Children whose birthdays occur earlier in the year enter school at an earlier age than students whose birthdays occur later in the year. For example, a child whose birthday occurs before the school year starts will begin kindergarten at age 5. However, a child whose birthday is in December will enter kindergarten the next year, when he/she is almost 6 years old. Assuming that the compulsory age that one can leave school is 16, then students whose birthdays fall earlier in the year can leave school before entering 10th grade, whereas those whose birthdays fall later in the year must remain in school for an additional few months. In examining the relationship between years of schooling and earnings for men who are likely to leave school when they reach the compulsory school age, birth date is a good instrument because it determines who starts school in a given year or a year later, but is not correlated with omitted variables. Compulsory schooling laws derived from the states in which individuals were born are also a good instrument because they determine who can leave school in a given year or a year later but are probably uncorrelated with ability or family background. Angrist and Krueger explain this as follows: "The intuition behind instrumental variables in this case is that differences in earnings by quarter of birth are assumed to be accounted for solely by differences in schooling by quarter of birth. . . . Only a small part of the variability in schooling—the part associated with quarter of birth—is used to identify the return to education" (p. 74). In this example, the estimated earning gain from more time in school applies to those who are likely to leave school at the minimum leaving age. It might not apply to those who are college bound or who are determined to finish high school even if they could leave school at age 16. In order to test the same hypothesis for other groups, another instrument would have to be found, or different survey data collected.

Angrist and Krueger (1995) found that men born in the first quarter of the year have about one tenth of a year less schooling and earned about 0.1% less than men born later in the year, but this difference was negligible. As it turns out, instrumental variables estimates using the Angrist and Krueger quarter of birth instruments are remarkably similar to the corresponding regression estimates that make no adjustment for unobservables. The investigators therefore concluded that there is no omitted variables bias in standard regression models estimating the effects of education on earnings.[30]

As Currie (2003) observes, there are several difficulties with using instrumental variables to correct for bias resulting from omitted variables. From a pragmatic standpoint, it is quite difficult to identify good instruments. Moreover, although the analyst can check to see whether different instrumental variables produce consistent results, it is not possible to check the validity of one's assumptions about the variables. In addition, instrumental variables may be only weakly related to the endogenous variable; the use of such "weak" instruments can result in biased and misleading estimates (Currie; see also Staiger and Stock, 1997, and Bound, Jaeger, and Baker, 1995, for a discussion of weak instruments; Angrist and Krueger, 1995, show that the estimates in their 1991 article are not affected by this problem).

Propensity Scores

A third method used to correct for selection bias is propensity scores. An important difference between propensity score methods and instrumental variables methods is that the former can correct for omitted variables bias due to unobserved characteristics while the latter corrects only for bias from observed characteristics or covariates. Propensity-score methods essentially are a version of regression or matching that allows researchers to focus on the observed covariates that "matter most."

Most regression analyses in nonrandomized observational studies are carried out for the full range of a particular sample, without regard for the probability that individuals have of being in the treatment or control groups. Propensity score matching is a technique developed by Rosenbaum and Rubin (1983) to represent the predicted probability that individuals with certain characteristics would be assigned to a treatment group when assignment is nonrandom (see also Rubin, 1997). The advantage of using propensity score matching is that it aggregates a number of characteristics that individually would be difficult to match among those in the treatment and non-treatment groups. Take the example of student performance in private schools compared to public schools. Students from disadvantaged families are much less likely to attend private schools. At the other end of the spectrum, students from well-off families, particularly minority high-income families, have a relatively higher probability of attending a private school. To approach a random assignment trial, we should compare individuals who have a reasonable probability of choosing to be in either the treatment (e.g., private school) or the control group (e.g., public school). Students with similar propensities to be in the treatment group (whether they are in the treatment group or not) can be matched on the basis of their propensity scores. The difference in their achievement scores would be closer to the difference we would expect in a random assignment of students to the two groups, since it is much more likely that their pretreatment characteristics are similar.

There are a number of ways propensity scores can be used to match students in the treatment and control groups (in this instance, private and public schools). Perhaps the most common way is to sort students from each group into "bins" or strata based on the distribution of propensity scores. Within each bin, the characteristics of students in the two treatment conditions are similar on a weighted composite of observed covariates. If the average characteristics of students within a bin are not equal, a more refined model is developed, using additional bins or strata until a balance in the characteristics of students in each group (e.g., public and private schools) is achieved. In some cases, there may be "bins" in which there is no overlap between the treatment and control groups, indicating that these individuals (e.g., students at the ends of the spectrum mentioned above) have virtually no probability of attending private schools on the low end or public schools on the high end. Because these students have no matches, they are excluded from analyses. This technique approximates randomized assignment since students within each of the remaining bins or strata have a roughly equal probability (based on their aggregate characteristics) of being selected into either the treatment or control condition.[31]

Propensity scores address an important issue in empirical research, namely, estimates of effects for certain groups when randomization is not possible, and where sample elements have self-selected themselves into treatment or control conditions.

> All statistical methods, from the simplest regressions to the most complex structural models, have elements of this limitation when used to analyze phenomena with heterogeneous responses. Nevertheless, many interventions and relationships can be fruitfully studied using

estimated effects for specific subsamples, provided the possible limitations to generalizing the results are understood and explored. Indeed, this lack of immediate generality is probably the norm in medical research based on clinical trials, yet much progress has been made in that field. (Angrist & Krueger, 2001, p. 78)

Stephen Morgan (2001) addressed the issue of observable differences in the nonrandom assignment of students to Catholic and public secondary schools. Using data from the National Education Longitudinal Study, he estimated a Catholic school effect on 12th-grade achievement. He also estimated the propensity of Catholic and public school students to attend Catholic schools based on a set of socioeconomic and demographic variables, as well as the student's score on a 10th-grade achievement test; these propensity scores were used to match students attending Catholic and public schools. Morgan then re-estimated the Catholic school effect on mathematics and reading scores for matched groups of students; he also estimated the effect within propensity score strata. Since not all Catholic school students had a match in the sample of public school students at the upper end of the propensity to attend Catholic school (high-socioeconomic-class students), Morgan conducted two sets of estimates: one that included the unmatched students and one that did not. His findings suggest that the estimated Catholic school effect for those currently attending Catholic schools using propensity score matching is larger than the estimate without propensity score matching and is statistically significant even when non-matched students are omitted. Hong and Raudenbush (2005) also used propensity score matching to estimate the effects of kindergarten retention (versus promotion) on students' reading and mathematics achievement at the end of the retention year. This study is described in detail in Section 4.

In contrast to fixed effects and instrumental variables, propensity score matching adjusts only for *observed* characteristics. Because a large number of background characteristics are used in calculating propensity scores, the probability that a relevant variable has been omitted from analysis is reduced, though not eliminated. However, it is possible to test the sensitivity of results to hypothesized omitted variables (Rosenbaum & Rubin, 1983; Rosenbaum, 1986, 2002). Because an aggregate of characteristics is used in computing propensity scores, and analytic samples are restricted to individuals (or schools) that can be matched across treatment conditions, this approach to approximating randomized assignment is more effective when large, nationally representative datasets are used. The samples on which these datasets are based are sufficiently large to allow for analyses of a subsample and contain comprehensive information on the background characteristics of students and schools. If selection into the analysis is unbiased (e.g., exclusions due to missing data do not result in differences between the analysis sample and the larger sample), these results are also generalizable to the larger population of students or schools.

Regression Discontinuity

A fourth method that can be used to approximate random assignment is regression discontinuity.[32] Regression discontinuity also plays on features of certain occurrences in education that have the qualities of a natural experiment; namely, when group members are subject to a treatment because they fall either above or below a certain cutoff score (for recent examples of this approach, see Cook, in press; Hahn, Todd, & Van der Klaauw, 1999, 2001; Van der Klaauw, 2002). The example used in Campbell's (1969) seminal article on regression discontinuity is the effect of National Merit Scholarships on later income. The fact that those just above or below the cutoff for acceptance into the program are likely to be similar on a set of unobserved variables that predict scores on the test determining National Merit Scholarship awards suggests that the effect of the treatment on a dependent variable (in this case, future income) could be estimated by comparing this restricted group—those just above the cutoff (who received the treatment)—with those just below the cutoff (who did not receive the treatment). Campbell argued that "if the assignment mechanism used to award scholarships is discontinuous, for example, there is a threshold value of past achievement that determines whether an award is made, then one can control for any smooth function of past achievement and still estimate the effect of the award at the point of discontinuity" (Angrist & Lavy, 1999, p. 548). Assuming that individuals in this restricted group approximate a random assignment to the treatment and control groups (at this particular cutoff point), the estimate of regression at the cutoff point yields an unbiased estimate of the treatment. If there are situations in which there are multiple discontinuities, this provides an even better estimate of the treatment effect since it would then be estimated across a broader range of the initial independent variable (in the merit scholarship case, at different levels of test scores).

Another example of a regression discontinuity analysis is a study conducted by Brian Jacob and Lars Lefgren (2004) that compares remedial summer school and grade retention effects on cohorts of third- and sixth-grade students by using data from the Chicago Public Schools. Jacob and Lefgren limit their analysis of the effects over time of summer school and grade retention on relatively low-achieving students. To determine whether attending summer school and having to repeat a grade had a significant effect on reading and mathematics achievement, they compared students who were just above or below the cutoff for promotion to the next grade. The assumption was that low-achieving students who just barely exceeded the cutoff score for promotion would be similar to students who fell just below the cutoff for promotion; however, one group of students would receive the "treatment" (attending summer school and potentially having to repeat a grade), while the other would not. One year after the initial promotion decision, the third graders who barely failed to meet the promotional standard scored roughly 20% of a year's worth of learning higher than their peers who barely passed the standard. The effects faded somewhat by Year 2 but were still statistically significant. For sixth graders, the effects were not positive, although the authors note that the results for these students were confounded by the differential incentives that retained and promoted students faced in subsequent years.

Regression discontinuity designs require that samples be restricted to students who fall just above or below the cutoff point; thus analyses based on large-scale datasets have a greater likelihood of detecting treatment effects. In contrast to propensity score matching, where students are matched on the basis of aggregate characteristics, regression discontinuity *assumes* that students in the two groups have similar characteristics; however the validity of this assumption should be checked.

Implications of These Results for Causal Inference

The methods being used by social scientists in analyzing large datasets address key issues in educational policy—for example, the effect of attending a public or Catholic school, the effect of teachers on student achievement, the effect of program participation on earnings—and also address the selection bias that is inherent in nonrandom assignment. The studies reviewed here have carefully analyzed the sources of bias and a series of estimation problems in the datasets. The main point of discussing these different methods and their applications to a number of different policy problems in education is to show how large datasets that are not based on randomized assignment to treatment and control groups can be used to obtain unbiased estimates of treatment effects.

It should be clear from this discussion that there are important limits to survey analysis even when adjustments for selection bias and multiple levels of analysis are used. Since populations are heterogeneous, estimates of the relationship between an intervention and educational outcomes corrected for selection bias may not be applicable to groups that have a low probability of falling into either the treatment or control group. Even so, almost all of the studies cited were able to deal with the effects on different groups. Currie and Thomas (1999) estimated the effects of Head Start participation on Hispanic students, for example, and Morgan (2001) estimated the effect of attending Catholic school by social class. Some of these studies reinforce other studies that used different methods but reached similar conclusions. After two decades of discussion, for example, the Morgan analysis of the effect of attending Catholic secondary schools concludes that the effect of the treatment (attending a Catholic school) is positive and significant with respect to achievement, but this effect is not necessarily a consequence of a school's religious status as Catholic. This is also the conclusion reached a decade earlier by Bryk, Lee, and Holland (1993), who described a "Catholic school effect" as being associated with shared values, a moral imperative, and school policies rather than religiosity per se.

In the last few years, analyses of large-scale datasets using the methods described above have produced several important findings, some of which have implications for causal inference and for the design of randomized experiments. In the next section, we highlight several NSF-supported research studies that relied on large-scale datasets and were designed either to estimate causal effects or to provide the preliminary evidence necessary in designing randomized controlled experiments of educational interventions and identifying populations most likely to benefit from them.

Chapter 3 Notes

21 Researchers, however, have consistently recommended that randomized control trials can and should be embedded within large-scale
observational studies.

22 This is an example of the problem of *endogeneity*. This term refers to
the fact that an independent variable (e.g., charter school attendance)
is potentially a choice variable that is correlated with an unobserved
characteristic (e.g., parent motivation), or is itself caused in some
way by the outcome (e.g., student achievement). Strictly speaking,
endogeneity requires this feedback; otherwise, the problem is one
of omitted variables bias. As in the example above, a student's prior
achievement may influence parents' decision to send or not send
their child to a charter school. Once this initial decision is made, the
student's achievement may, in turn, influence the parents' decision to
have the child remain in or exit the school. In such cases, the outcome
is observed for both public and charter school students. This differs
from Heckman's classic example of sample selection bias where the
outcome is observed only for those who choose to participate in a
particular program. Heckman's two-step procedure is designed to
deal with this truncated distribution.

23 Propensity score matching controls only for observable characteristics, whereas the other methods control for both observed and
unobserved characteristics; however, in the case of propensity score
matching, sensitivity analysis can be used to test for the possible
effects of unobserved variables (Rosenbaum & Rubin, 1983; Rosenbaum, 1986, 2002).

24 Fixed effects models in this and the next example do not refer to fixed
effects as opposed to random effects assumptions that are applied in
a general linear model.

25 Students in the third grade in 1996, 1997, 1998, 1999, and 2002 were
followed until they left the North Carolina public school system,
completed the eighth grade, or until the 2001–2002 academic year,
whichever came first.

26 As the authors note, the drawback of this method is that it is not
based on the full population of charter school students. The authors
conducted additional analyses to determine whether the subsample

of students for whom test scores were available in both charter schools and regular public schools differed from the larger group of all charter school students in the grades observed. Although some differences between samples were found (e.g., the subsample over-represented charter school students who exited charter schools and underrepresented students who entered charter schools), the average impact of charter schools across all charter school students remained negative.

27 The authors used multiple approaches in estimating the effects of charter schools on charter school students and compared results across approaches; we have focused only on the individual fixed effects model.

28 If the instrumental variable itself is correlated with the omitted variable or the outcome variable, then it will bias the estimated effect of the independent variable (e.g., years of schooling) on the outcome.

29 This two-step procedure does not generate the correct standard errors; in practice, 2SLS software packages should be used for instrumental variables estimation so that the resulting statistical inferences are correct.

30 Many of the studies described in this report have been the subject of some controversy. The designs and methods that researchers use have both strengths and weaknesses. Limitations exist in nearly all studies, whether experimental or observational, making it incumbent upon the investigator to acknowledge such limitations and explore alternative explanations for their results.

31 An alternative method uses propensity scores to weight all observations to reflect the probabilities that individuals could be in the treatment and control groups and then estimates the treatment effect on the basis of observations weighted by their propensity scores.

32 Cook (in press) has recently written an article in which he argues that when a regression discontinuity design is perfectly implemented and the selection process is fully observed, an unbiased causal inference can be made from the model that is produced. In the article he reviews the history of regression discontinuity designs and the assumptions that were made in its development. The article outlines when these designs can be used and why this method is superior to other known causal methods, including its strengths and limitations for estimating causal inference.

4. Analysis of Large-Scale Datasets: Examples of NSF-Supported Research

NSF FUNDS A VARIETY OF STUDIES designed to investigate how to improve learning, especially in mathematics and science, including experiments, quasi-experiments, and secondary analyses of observational data.[33] Some of the studies focus on theory building, while others are evaluations where the researcher is interested in assessing the effectiveness of specific large-scale initiatives, such as systemic reform. We reviewed the research portfolio of NSF's Education and Human Resource Directorate and selected four quantitative studies that used different statistical techniques to investigate causal questions. These techniques serve as examples for investigators conducting secondary analyses of these and other large-scale datasets. All four studies address issues of causality. However, only the first two allow for causal inferences. We have included the other two studies because they can be used to generate causal hypotheses that can inform the design of experiments.

The first study, "How Large Are Teacher Effects?" examines teacher effects on student achievement based on data from the Tennessee Class Size Experiment, an experiment with random assignment (Nye, Konstantopoulos, & Hedges, 2004). Although the second study, "Effects of Kindergarten

Retention Policy on Children's Cognitive Growth in Reading and Mathematics," is based on observational data from the Early Childhood Longitudinal Study (ECLS), it approximates an experiment on the effects of kindergarten retention on children's literacy (Hong & Raudenbush, 2005). Using data from the Third International Mathematics and Science Study (TIMSS), the third study, *Why Schools Matter: A Cross-National Comparison of Curriculum and Learning,* employs multiple analytic approaches, including structural modeling, to uncover possible causal relationships between aspects of curriculum and achievement gains in mathematics and science (Schmidt et al., 2001). This study provides a strong foundation on which to construct an experiment with random assignment on the effects of curriculum on student learning. The last study, "The Role of Gender and Friendship in Advanced Course-Taking," uses standard regression techniques to examine the influence of friends on high school students' advanced course-taking in mathematics and science, using data from the National Longitudinal Study of Adolescent Health (Riegle-Crumb, Farkas, & Muller, 2006).

Case I. An Experiment With Random Assignment: "How Large Are Teacher Effects?"

To investigate teacher effects on student learning outcomes, Nye, Konstantopoulos, and Hedges (2004) conducted a secondary analysis of data from the Tennessee Class Size Experiment, or Project STAR (Student-Teacher Achievement Ratio), an experiment in which students and teachers were randomly assigned within each school to classes that varied in size and in the presence of a teacher aide (small classes, regular classes, and regular classes with a teacher aide). The original experiment was designed to compare the effects of class size and student-teacher ratios on student achievement (Finn & Achilles, 1990, 1999). In analyzing data from this experiment, Nye and her colleagues take advantage of the study's large sample and use of random assignment to compare the learning outcomes of students in the same treatment condition who had different teachers. In contrast to most research on teacher effects, which tends to be based on observational data and relies on statistical controls to correct for selection bias, Nye et al.'s use of data from an experiment with random assignment of both students and teachers allows them to draw causal inferences about teacher effects on student achievement with a high degree of confidence.

Research Question and Theoretical Frame

Specifically, Nye and her colleagues use data from Project STAR to determine whether there are teacher effects on student achievement and to estimate the magnitude of these effects. If teacher effects are large, they argue, then identifying factors that contribute to teacher effectiveness would be important to both education researchers and reformers. If these effects are small, then finding ways to improve teacher effectiveness would be a less promising reform strategy.

Researchers have differed in their perspectives on what factors contribute to teacher effectiveness and whether differences in teacher quality have significant effects on student learning outcomes. Some have assumed that teacher and school characteristics such as teacher experience and education, class size, and school resources may affect the quality of teaching and in turn student achievement. Others argue that these measured characteristics have little effect on student learning, but acknowledge that there may be other observed or unobserved characteristics that have significant effects on student learning outcomes.

Problems With Studies of Teacher Effectiveness

Although a considerable number of studies have been conducted on teacher effects, results have been mixed. Some studies indicate that teacher effects are negligible; others suggest that characteristics such as teacher experience and education have significant effects on student achievement (for reviews of the literature, see Hanushek, 1986, and Greenwald, Hedges, & Laine, 1996). However, reviewers of these studies generally agree that it is difficult to draw causal inferences about the relationship between measures of teacher quality and student achievement because of the exclusion of potentially relevant variables such as teacher instructional practices. Nye and her colleagues are able to avoid these problems of selection bias by using data from an experiment with random assignment.

Nye et al. identify two traditions of research on teacher effectiveness and describe the limitations of each with respect to making causal inferences. One tradition, referred to as education production-function studies, examines the relationship between specific teacher or school characteristics (e.g., teacher experience, teacher education, class size) and student achievement. These school resource variables tend to be associated with student and family characteristics because parents typically choose the neighborhoods they live in (and the schools within them) based on particular preferences and resources. Although production-function studies attempt to adjust statistically for these associations by including student and family characteristics in the analyses, they fail to take into account the possible influences of unmeasured characteristics on student learning outcomes (e.g., instructional practices) and often include measures that may have no relation to student achievement (e.g., teacher salary). In many studies, determining the direction of causality between teacher effectiveness and student achievement is also problematic because the assignment of students to classes is often based on student and teacher characteristics. For example, more experienced teachers may be assigned to classes of high-achieving students as a reward for seniority, making it difficult to determine whether learning outcomes are due to teacher effects or students' prior achievement.

Studies in the second tradition examine variations in student achievement across classrooms, adjusting for student background characteristics. These studies typically include a prior measure of student achievement, making the focus of the analysis variation in student achievement gains across classrooms. It is assumed that between-classroom variation in student achievement gains is caused by differences in teacher effectiveness. These analyses, however, may fail to include adequate adjustments for preexisting differences between students assigned to different classrooms (i.e., selection bias), including unobserved differences related to achievement growth (e.g., differences in the quality of instruction students received in prior years).

Experimental Design: Avoiding Problems of Selection Bias

The randomized assignment of students and teachers to treatment conditions, and to classrooms within treatment conditions, ensures that any differences between groups in participants' pretreatment characteristics occur only by chance. Because both teachers and students were randomly assigned to treatment conditions, Nye and colleagues can assume that, barring any difficulties in implementing the experiment, any significant differences in student achievement across treatment conditions can be attributed to either treatment effects (class size and the presence or absence of a teacher aide) or teacher effects; within classrooms of the same type (e.g., small), these differences can be attributed to teacher effects.

Even though experiments are designed to produce valid evidence of causal effects, they are not always implemented with fidelity (e.g., students may move between treatment groups after being randomly assigned, or there may be differential attrition across treatment groups). Nye and her colleagues therefore investigated deviations from the study design and their potential effects on study outcomes. They also conducted tests to determine whether randomization had been effective in eliminating systematic differences between treatment groups. Although randomized assignment tends to produce treatment groups that are, on average, balanced with respect to pretreatment characteristics, within any single trial, randomization may result in groups that systematically differ with respect to certain pretreatment characteristics.

Study Design, Data, and Approach

The Tennessee Class Size Experiment was a 4-year longitudinal study, initially fielded in 1985, that was funded by the Tennessee legislature and conducted by the state department of education. More than 6,000 students from 79 schools and 42 school districts in Tennessee participated in the first year of study, and almost 12,000 students participated over the course of the 4-year experiment (Finn & Achilles, 1999). The policy issue addressed by the study was the effect of class size on student learning. Specifically, the study examined whether reducing the number of students in a single classroom, or reducing class size by having two adults in the classroom, improved students' mathematics and reading achievement more than "regular-sized" classes. Unlike previous studies of the effects of class size on student achievement, this study was a controlled experiment with random assignment.

Within each school, entering kindergarten students were randomly assigned to one of three types of classrooms: small classes (13–17 students), regular classes (22–26 students), or regular classes with a full-time teacher aide. Teachers were also randomly assigned to these three treatment conditions.

Student assignments by classroom type were maintained throughout the day and throughout the school year. Students who entered a school in first grade or in subsequent grades were randomly assigned to classroom type upon entry. As students in the experimental cohort progressed through subsequent grade levels, teachers at each grade level were randomly assigned to one of the three types of classrooms each year. Agreements were obtained from school districts to remain in the study for 4 years and to maintain the random assignment of students to classroom type from kindergarten through third grade.[34]

In analyzing data from the Tennessee Class Size Experiment, Nye et al. focused on differences in the mathematics and reading achievement of students in different classrooms within the same treatment condition. Due to the large size of the dataset, the researchers were able to select a subset of schools that had at least two classrooms assigned to the same treatment condition.[35] In analyzing variations in math and reading achievement, they examined differences in both achievement status (e.g., achievement measured at a particular grade level) and achievement gains (e.g., achievement growth from one grade to the next).[36]

Analyses and Results

In the original experiment, the fidelity with which the study was implemented was somewhat compromised. In a small number of cases there was overlap in the sizes of the classes categorized as large and small. In kindergarten and later grades, there was also a small amount of crossover of students between classroom types. There was some student attrition between kindergarten and third grade as well. Preliminary analyses were therefore conducted to investigate deviations from the study design; based on these analyses, the investigators concluded that none of the deviations invalidated the results of the original experiment.[37] Additional checks were conducted to ensure that randomization had been effective in eliminating preexisting differences between students and teachers assigned to different types of classrooms. Results of these checks were consistent with successful randomization. For example, no differences were found in the SES, ethnicity, or age of students across treatment conditions. Analyses also revealed no systematic differences in these characteristics across classrooms within the same treatment condition within schools.[38]

Because Nye et al.'s study focuses on variation in student achievement across teachers within the same treatment group (small class, regular class, regular class with teacher aide), a method of analysis was needed that took into account the clustering of students within classrooms, treatment groups, and schools. Hierarchical linear modeling (Bryk & Raudenbush, 2002) was therefore used in analyzing teacher effects on student achievement. This method of analysis allowed the investigators to examine between-classroom but within-school-and-treatment variation in reading and mathematics achievement. Within a school, systematic variation in student achievement between classes in the same treatment condition could be attributed to teacher effects.[39]

To estimate teacher effects on student achievement, Nye and her colleagues developed separate analytic models to examine teacher effects on achievement gains and on achievement status. Separate models were also constructed for reading and mathematics achievement for each grade level. Results of these analyses showed that variations in student achievement gains between classrooms (and thus teachers) within the same treatment condition were significantly larger than variations in student achievement gains between schools, indicating that the teacher a student is assigned to may be more important for that student's achievement than the school the student attends. This pattern of results was similar for reading and mathematics achievement and was consistent across grades, indicating that teachers had substantial effects on student learning growth from one year to the next.[40] Teacher effects were found to be much larger in mathematics than in reading, regardless of the grade attended.[41] Nye et al. suggest that mathematics is more likely to be learned in school and thus to be influenced by teachers, whereas reading is often learned in contexts other than school; alternatively, there may be more variation (either in quantity or quality) of mathematics instruction than in reading instruction. Teacher effects on student achievement status were found to be similar in magnitude to those for achievement gains.[42]

Additional analyses were conducted to determine whether teacher effects might be explained by differences in teacher experience or education and whether these effects varied with school or student SES. Results indicated that teacher experience and education explained very little of the variance in teacher effects (never more than 5%). However, teacher effects did vary significantly by school SES; there was more variation in teacher effects in low-SES schools than in high-SES schools. The proportion of total variance in student achievement accounted for by teacher effects was also higher in low-SES schools.[43] These findings suggest that teacher effects are much more uneven in low-SES versus high-SES schools. Thus, in low-SES schools, which teacher a student is assigned to has a greater impact on average classroom achievement than it does in high-SES schools. In analyzing the relationship between teacher effects and student SES, the investigators found that although teacher effects vary by student SES, this variation does not help to explain variation in teachers' effectiveness across schools.

Implications for Estimating Causal Effects

This study analyzes data from a randomized controlled experiment in which students and teachers within each school were randomly assigned to treatment conditions (small class, regular class, regular class with teacher aide). Because random assignment was used, all observed or unobserved differences in teacher and student characteristics across treatment conditions occur by chance alone, making it unnecessary to adjust for specific student or family characteristics or to specify in advance teacher characteristics that are related to student achievement. Checks of differences between treatment groups confirmed that randomization was effective in eliminating systematic differences in the pretreatment characteristics of students (and teachers) assigned to different treatment conditions. Differences in student achievement across treatment conditions could thus be attributed to treatment effects rather than to the pretreatment characteristics of students or teachers.

By focusing on schools in which different teachers were assigned to the same treatment condition, Nye and her colleagues were able to differentiate between treatment effects and teacher effects. Because random assignment was used, within any given school, systematic variation in achievement between classrooms within the same treatment condition could be attributed to teacher effects. The investigators were thus able to draw causal inferences about teacher effects on student achievement.

As Nye and her colleagues observe, their results suggest that

> teacher effects are real and are of a magnitude that is consistent with that estimated in previous studies. However, we would argue that, because of random assignment of teachers and students to classrooms in this experiment, our results provide stronger evidence

about teacher effects. The results of this study support the idea that there are substantial differences among teachers in the ability to produce achievement gains in their students . . . [suggesting] that interventions to improve the effectiveness of teachers or identify effective teachers might be promising strategies for improving student achievement. (p. 253)

The authors acknowledge that "this design cannot identify the specific characteristics that are responsible for teacher effectiveness" (p. 239). Although both teacher education and teacher experience were examined, they explained virtually none of the variance in teacher effects. Because Nye et al. were analyzing data that were collected for a different purpose (i.e., to examine the relationship between class size and student achievement), their analysis was constrained by the available data on teacher characteristics.

That there are teacher effects on student achievement may seem obvious. However, demonstrating these effects empirically using data from an experimental study is an important contribution. We can be confident that there are substantial teacher effects and that they vary by school SES. These findings suggest that interventions to replace less qualified teachers or to improve teacher quality would be more promising in low-SES schools than in high-SES schools. Overall, the study addresses issues of data quality, provides stronger grounds on which to base policy decisions, and suggests strategies for designing future intervention studies. It also suggests possibilities for conducting analyses of data from experimental studies. As randomized controlled experiments become more common in education, data from these studies will provide additional opportunities for secondary analyses.

Case II. Approximating a Randomized Experiment: "Effects of Kindergarten Retention Policy on Children's Cognitive Growth in Reading and Mathematics"

To investigate the causal effects of kindergarten retention policies on children's cognitive growth in mathematics and reading, Hong and Raudenbush (2005) use observational data from the Early Childhood Longitudinal Study (ECLS-K), to approximate a randomized controlled experiment. Using propensity score matching, they construct treatment groups from this national dataset that are comparable with respect to students' probabilities of being retained and balanced with respect to students' pretreatment characteristics. A similar analysis is conducted at the school level to examine the effects of school retention policies (allowing or banning retention) on student learning outcomes.

Research Questions and Theoretical Frame

The purpose of this study is to determine whether kindergartners who were retained would have had higher growth rates in reading and mathematics if they had been promoted to first grade. In other words, if an experiment could be conducted in which kindergartners were randomly assigned to treatment groups (retention and promotion), would the growth trajectories of retained students differ significantly from those of promoted students? Similarly, if schools could be randomly assigned to policy conditions (allowing or banning retention), would the learning outcomes of students in retention schools differ significantly from those in nonretention schools?

Developmental psychologists differ in their perspectives on the potential benefits of kindergarten retention. Proponents of retention argue that children develop at different rates; kindergartners who have trouble keeping up academically may need additional time to mature socially and cognitively before being entering first grade (Plummer & Graziano, 1987; Smith & Shepherd, 1988). This perspective suggests that kindergarten retention would have a positive effect on the learning outcomes of children who are retained because they would be given additional time to master concepts and skills that their classmates have already mastered. Children who are promoted may also benefit by being in classrooms with students who have similar levels of academic achievement instead of in classrooms that vary widely in achievement levels, assuming that retained students have substantially lower levels of achievement than those who are promoted (Byrnes, 1989; see also Smith & Shepard for a review). Since both retained and promoted students would potentially benefit from a policy of retention, the average learning growth of students in retention schools should be higher than that of students in nonretention schools.

Other developmental psychologists contend that having children repeat an unsuccessful learning experience is more likely to impede than enhance students' cognitive and social development (Morrison, Griffith, & Alberts, 1997). It has been argued that retention stigmatizes students, leading to lower parent, teacher, and self- expectations (Jackson, 1975; Shephard, 1989). Supporters of eliminating retention maintain that reforming instructional practices to correct children's learning difficulties may be more effective than retention in improving the learning outcomes of retained students (Karweit, 1992; Leinhardt, 1980; Reynolds, 1992; Tanner & Galis, 1997). At both the individual and school levels, retention is likely to have a negligible or negative effect on student learning.

Problems With Studies of Retention

Results of previous research on retention effects have been inconclusive. A large number of studies show a negative relationship between kindergarten retention and academic achievement or personal/social development (see, e.g., Holmes, 1989; Nagaoka & Roderick, 2004). A similarly large number of studies show no statistically significant relationship between retention and these outcomes (see, e.g., Shepard, 1989; Jimerson, 2001). Such inconsistencies appear to be due in part to weaknesses in study design. One common problem with previous retention studies is that researchers have not considered whether the retained and promoted groups are comparable (i.e., at similar risk for retention). Failure to control for observed differences between groups may have led investigators to draw invalid inferences about retention effects.

Two primary strategies have been used in past retention research: (a) same-grade comparisons, and (b) same-age comparisons. Same-grade studies, which constitute the majority of retention studies, compare the outcomes of students who are repeating a grade with those of students who are completing that grade for the first time. In same-age studies, the outcomes of retained children are compared with those of children of the same age who were promoted to the next grade. Both strategies are problematic with regard to drawing valid causal inferences about the effects of retention on children's academic progress. In the case of same-grade studies, researchers are able to compare the academic standing of children who are retained with that of their classmates both before and after retention but are unable to make inferences about how retained children might have performed had they been promoted to the next grade. In same-age studies, the outcomes of retained students are often compared with those of all promoted students, including those who had virtually no chance of being retained. These low-risk students provide no information on which to base inferences about how retained students might have performed if promoted. Such studies also typically rely on statistical adjustments for a limited number of background variables to equate groups. But when the groups are barely comparable with respect to their probability of being retained, this technique is unlikely to produce valid results.

Studies that restrict their comparisons of retained students to low-achieving students who have been promoted are more promising with respect to drawing causal inferences because these were students who were at risk for retention in the previous year and thus are more likely to be similar to the students who were actually retained. To adjust for any remaining differences between retained and promoted groups, however, researchers typically adjust for only a few background characteristics. Most do not adjust for prior learning growth rate, a variable that needs to be included if valid inferences are to be made about differences in the academic progress of the two groups. Most of these studies also assume that all background characteristics associated with retention have been included in the analysis, an assumption that typically is unwarranted.

Constructing a comparison group by matching students on background characteristics has the advantage of making differences between groups more readily apparent (e.g., the extent to which there is overlap between the groups with respect to the risk of being retained). However, most studies using this approach have been able to match on only a limited number of characteristics, raising questions about the initial equivalence of the matched groups. In addition, none of the studies have compared the academic achievement or social development of retained students with these outcomes for matched peers who were promoted.

Conducting a randomized controlled experiment designed to study retention effects would be problematic, as it is unlikely that parents would allow their child to be retained or promoted on a random basis (e.g., irrespective of their grades, ability, and social development). If it is not feasible to randomly assign students to treatment conditions (retention or promotion), how can a randomized experiment be approximated?

If the goal is to determine whether retained students would
have performed better if they had been promoted, then the
outcomes of retained students need to be compared to those
of promoted students who have similar characteristics, including similar probabilities of being retained. Some mechanism is
needed to construct comparison or treatment groups that are
balanced with respect to background characteristics. Propensity score matching, the method used by Hong and Raudenbush, provides this mechanism.

Controlling for Selection Bias: Propensity Score Matching

Propensity score methods approximate randomized assignment to treatment conditions by ensuring that students have
equivalent chances of being in the retained or in the promoted
group. Because groups are comparable in terms of their pretreatment characteristics, any differences in the learning outcomes of the two groups can be attributed to differences in
treatment (retention versus promotion). As a result, the cognitive growth of promoted students can be interpreted as indicating how retained students might have performed if they
had been promoted instead.

An advantage of propensity score methods is that they
estimate each student's probability of being retained based
on an aggregate of characteristics. Being able to summarize
these characteristics in one composite measure (the propensity score) makes it possible for analysts to make a straightforward assessment of whether there is sufficient overlap between
groups to justify comparison and to match students based on
their propensity scores when there is sufficient overlap (Rosenbaum & Rubin, 1983; Rubin 1997). Propensity score matching is facilitated by using large-scale nationally representative
datasets such as ECLS.[44]

Propensity score matching adjusts for systematic differences in the characteristics of the observed groups in two

ways: (a) by eliminating students who have virtually no probability of being retained (high-achieving students, for example, may have almost no chance of being retained and offer no useful information on which to base estimates of the learning outcomes of retained and promoted students who are at similar risk for retention); and (b) by matching the remaining students in each group on the basis of characteristics known to be associated with retention.

To construct a propensity score model, in this case for kindergarten retention, the analyst first identifies variables that are systematically associated with retention using bivariate analysis. These variables are then included as predictors of kindergarten retention in multivariate regression models. Because many of the variables are associated with each other, only some of them will have a significant association with retention when all variables are included in the model, allowing the analyst to reduce the number of variables used in propensity models. These significant predictors are used to calculate propensity scores for students in the retained and promoted groups. By stratifying and matching students in each group on the basis of their propensity scores, analysts can identify students for whom there are no matches and exclude them from analysis. Students for whom matches are found will have similar characteristics.

Study Design, Data, and Approach

Hong and Raudenbush conduct three analyses. The first identifies the factors associated with student retention. The second estimates how retained students would have performed in reading and mathematics if they had instead been promoted. The third analysis estimates the effects of the school's retention policy (allowing or banning retention) on students' cognitive growth in reading and mathematics; this analysis was conducted at the level of the school rather than the student.

Thus school characteristics associated with the adoption of a retention policy were identified and used to calculate school propensity scores, using the same series of steps described for calculating student propensity scores.

Of the more than 20,000 first-time kindergartners included in the ECLS study, there are 13,520 for whom retention/promotion information is available. Information on kindergarten retention policies is also available for 1,221 schools in the study. Due to missing data on kindergarten retention policies, 1,667 students were excluded from the analyses.[45] After exclusions, the analysis sample consisted of 471 retained kindergartners and 10,255 promoted students in 1,080 retention schools, and 1,117 promoted students in 141 nonretention schools. For most students, mathematics and reading assessment data were obtained during the fall and spring of the kindergarten year and the spring of the following year.[46] The ECLS dataset also contains extensive information on the background characteristics of students obtained through parent, teacher, and school administrator surveys.

Analyses and Results

Using bivariate analysis, Hong and Raudenbush initially identified 207 student characteristics that were associated with retention based on prior research. When these variables were included in multivariate regression analyses, 39 of them were found to be significant predictors of retention. For example, children from single-parent families with several siblings, those whose parents had a lower commitment to parenting, and those who had lower scores on kindergarten assessments had a greater likelihood of being retained. Teacher perceptions were also found to be significant predictors of retention. Students who were retained were more likely to be placed in the lowest reading group in kindergarten (based on the teacher's perception of the child's reading ability) and were rarely able to move into a higher reading group.[47]

This set of predictors was used to calculate a propensity score for each student in the observed retention and promotion groups (i.e., each student's probability of being retained based on this combined set of characteristics). Propensity scores of students in the two groups were then examined to ensure that the distributions overlapped. No matches were found for 3,087 students in retention schools who had virtually no chance of being retained, and these students were excluded from the analyses. The remaining students were stratified and matched on the basis of their propensity scores. This process resulted in retention and promotion groups that were balanced with respect to students' background characteristics and their probabilities of being retained, thus approximating the random assignment of students to treatment conditions.

Because students' potential learning outcomes are likely to depend on treatment setting (the school), hierarchical linear modeling (HLM) was used to estimate the effects of retention on students' reading and mathematics achievement. HLM adjusts for similarities among students who attend the same school and allows the analyst to examine variation in retention effects at both the student and school levels. Results of this analysis indicated that, on average, retained students had significantly lower growth trajectories in reading and mathematics than promoted students who were at similar risk for retention. If a retained student had instead been promoted, his or her expected achievement would be approximately 9 points higher in reading and 6 points higher in math at the end of the treatment year. The magnitude of these estimated effects was about two-thirds of a standard deviation of the outcome in both reading and mathematics, a difference equivalent to approximately a half-year's learning growth in each subject area.[48]

The HLM results also indicated that retention effects varied significantly across schools. The difference in the reading growth trajectories of retained and promoted students at similar risk of retention was greatest in schools with higher average reading achievement. In contrast, the difference in mathematics growth trajectories was greatest in schools with lower average mathematics achievement. The investigators suggest that curricular and instructional differences between kindergarten and first grade may account for these differences. In high-achieving schools, reading instruction typically occurs at a relatively fast pace. Students who are promoted may therefore learn at a faster rate than those who are retained. In low-achieving schools, the kindergarten curriculum often includes little mathematics content, providing retained students with fewer opportunities for learning growth relative to promoted students.[49]

In contrast to randomized assignment, which tends to create groups that are balanced with respect to observed and unobserved characteristics, propensity score matching takes into account only the observed characteristics of group members. The investigators therefore conducted an additional analysis to check for the sensitivity of their results to the inclusion of adjustments for unmeasured characteristics.[50] They found that these adjustments did not significantly affect their estimates of retention effects, suggesting that their results were not biased due to the exclusion of unobserved characteristics.

Taking their analysis a step further, the investigators estimated the overall impact of a school's retention policy (allowing or banning retention) on the average learning outcomes of students; they also estimated its impact on students who were likely to be promoted if retention were adopted. Propensity score methods and hierarchical linear modeling were again used to address these questions.[51] Results of these analyses indicated that adopting a kindergarten retention policy had no significant effect on students' average learning growth, nor did it have an effect on the learning growth of students who were likely to be promoted under the policy.

Implications for Estimating Causal Effects

The use of sophisticated statistical techniques, together with a comprehensive dataset based on a large, nationally representative sample, allows the investigators to draw causal inferences about the effects of kindergarten retention policies on student cognitive growth with a relatively high degree of confidence. They are able to make these causal inferences because propensity score matching effectively makes treatment group assignment independent of students' pretreatment characteristics, including their probability of being retained. Previous studies of retention effects that relied on conventional statistical methods often made unwarranted assumptions about the extent of overlap between comparison groups and typically adjusted for only a few background characteristics. In contrast, propensity score matching uses straightforward procedures for determining whether there is sufficient overlap between groups (e.g., with respect to the risk of being retained) and makes simultaneous adjustments for a large number of background characteristics.

A limitation of propensity score methods is that they can adjust only for observed differences in the background characteristics of group members. It is possible that a relevant variable, such as the onset of a serious illness, may have been omitted from the analysis. However, there are statistical techniques that can be used to test for the possible effects of omitted variables (Lin, Psaty, & Kronmal, 1998; Rosenbaum & Rubin, 1983; Rosenbaum, 1986, 2002).

Approximating a randomized controlled experiment with observational data allows the investigators to draw on the strengths of both experimental and observational designs. Because their analyses are based on data from a nationally representative sample of kindergartners and schools, they are able to describe the characteristics of students who were retained as well as the characteristics of schools that adopted a kindergarten retention policy; thus they can identify students and schools that are most likely to be affected by retention policies.

In addition to estimating the average effect of retention on the cognitive growth of retained students, the investigators are able to demonstrate variation in these effects across schools. Such school-to-school variation suggests that school characteristics, such as approaches to curriculum and instruction, may moderate the negative effects of retention; closer examination of such variation in future studies could prove useful in identifying the causal mechanisms through which retention and promotion affect students' cognitive growth.

Conducting a randomized controlled experiment to study retention effects is likely to be operationally difficult; it could also be argued that since the consequences of retention are inconclusive, subjecting students to an untested condition is unethical. Since a randomized experiment is not feasible in this instance, the investigators creatively use a large-scale national dataset to approximate an experimental design. Their study demonstrates that quasi-experiments can be very powerful if the datasets are well designed and comprehensive and contain reliable and valid measures of the variables of interest. More studies of this type are needed in investigating the effects of educational interventions, particularly in situations where randomized controlled experiments are not feasible.

Case III. Structural Modeling: *Why Schools Matter: A Cross-National Comparison of Curriculum and Learning*

Why Schools Matter (Schmidt et al., 2001) investigates the relationship between curriculum (content standards, textbooks, teacher coverage, and teacher instructional time) and learning using data from the Third International Mathematics and Science Study (TIMSS), a cross-national study of mathematics and science achievement. The authors define student learning as the gains in subject-specific competencies and knowledge over a 1-year period. Their focus on learning—systematic gains over time not due to maturation—leads them to explore achievement gains (the change in achievement from one time point to another) rather than achievement status (a measure of cumulative achievement up to a particular time point). Although the study is not experimental in design, the investigators' use of sophisticated statistical techniques allows them to generate causal hypotheses concerning specific aspects of the curriculum on student learning.

Research Questions and Theoretical Frame

Through an examination of cross-national variation in topic coverage in mathematics and science, Schmidt and his colleagues investigate the relationship between curriculum coverage and student learning gains in these subjects. Variation in topic coverage within individual countries and its relationship to student learning are also examined. The investigators' primary research questions are as follows: (a) To what extent do countries vary in their coverage of particular mathematics and science topics? (b) What is the relationship between topic coverage and student learning gains? and (c) Within individual countries, how does variation in topic coverage across schools and classrooms relate to differences in student learning outcomes?

　　　Research on curriculum and instruction indicates that what gets taught in school and how much time teachers devote to instruction affects student learning and achievement. Students' opportunities to learn are structured both by the content and organization of the curriculum and by the time teachers devote to specific topics of instruction. Research drawing on both the opportunity-to-learn paradigm (Sorenson, 1970, 1987) and organizational approaches to schooling (see, e.g., Bidwell, 1965, 2000; Bidwell, Frank, & Quiroz, 1997; Firestone, 1985; Ingersoll, 1993; Kilgore, 1991; Kilgore & Pendleton, 1993) has shown that curriculum and instruction are important factors in the stratification of student learning (see, e.g., Dreeben & Gamoran, 1986; Gamoran & Berends, 1988; Gamoran, 1989; Lee, Smith, & Croninger, 1997).

Recognizing the importance of the curriculum for student learning outcomes, policymakers have moved toward developing curricular content standards under the assumption that such standards ultimately will influence what is actually taught in schools. It is at this level that Schmidt and his colleagues enter the debate on curriculum and instruction and approach it as a problem of importance not only to the United States but also internationally. In conceptualizing the relationship between curriculum and student learning outcomes, they move beyond standard definitions of curriculum (teacher content coverage and instructional time) to include national content standards. They also expand their definition of content coverage to include textbook coverage, under the assumption that the textbooks that teachers use for instruction will influence their coverage of particular topics. Four aspects of the curriculum are thus identified in their conceptualization: content standards, textbook coverage, teacher coverage, and time devoted to instruction.

Problems With Research on Curriculum and Learning

As Schmidt et al. note, most studies of curriculum have been qualitative, and studies that have attempted to examine the relationship between curriculum and learning quantitatively have relied on teacher assessments of students' opportunities to learn material tapped by items on achievement tests. Such assessments are potentially biased and unreliable indicators of topic coverage. In devising measures of specific aspects of curriculum and in using multiple indicators of curriculum coverage, Schmidt and his colleagues are able to provide much stronger evidence linking curriculum and learning. They are also able to quantitatively assess and model the relationships among aspects of the curriculum and the relation of each to student achievement gains. Their use of curriculum-sensitive measurement within major content categories in turn increases the likelihood of finding curriculum effects and of finding effects that vary by topic.

By focusing on specific sets of topics and individual countries, the investigators are able to determine how emphasis on a particular topic varies across countries; they can also determine which topics constitute the core mathematics and science curriculum (e.g., in eighth grade) for the majority of countries participating in TIMSS. Within individual countries, they are able to determine the relative emphasis given to particular topics across classrooms and schools. The investigators observe that in "countries such as the U.S., where local control or even school control of the curriculum is the rule," one might expect large variations in curriculum coverage (and opportunities to learn) across schools, and thus large variations in student achievement.

Modeling the Potential Causal Effects of
Curriculum on Student Learning

The investigators develop and test a structural model of the relationships among specific aspects of the curriculum (content standards, textbook coverage, teacher coverage, and instructional time) and between each of these curricular aspects and student achievement.[52] As specified in the model, content standards are assumed to influence textbook coverage of specific topics and the selection of textbooks for use in classrooms. Similarly, content standards may affect teacher

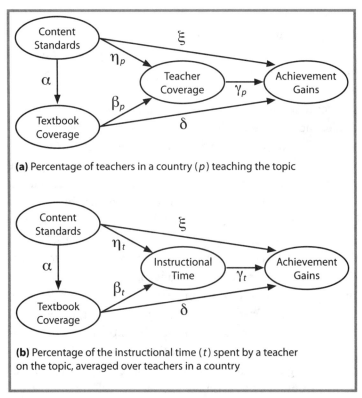

(a) Percentage of teachers in a country (p) teaching the topic

(b) Percentage of the instructional time (t) spent by a teacher on the topic, averaged over teachers in a country

Figure 1. *A structural model of relationships among curricular aspects and student learning. Adapted from Schmidt et al., 2001, p. 31, with permission from the author.*

coverage or the amount of instructional time devoted to particular topics through their role in teacher preparation and professional development. Textbook coverage of particular topics is also likely to affect teacher coverage of those topics (see Figure 1).

Each of these aspects of the curriculum (content standards, textbook coverage, teacher coverage, and instructional time) may relate to student learning either directly or indirectly. Direct relationships (often referred to as "direct effects") can be thought of as the simple path from content standards to learning, while the indirect relationships can be thought of as the compound path from content standards to textbook coverage to teacher coverage and instructional time to student learning. For example, the quality of textbooks as reflected in the content coverage of particular topics may directly affect student achievement gains for those topics, as well as indirectly affecting such gains through their effect on teacher coverage.

The investigators use this structural model to isolate the relationships among specific aspects of the curriculum on student learning outcomes. They do not attempt to draw causal inferences about these effects. Rather, they conceptually model and statistically evaluate the potential causal effects of specific aspects of the curriculum on student learning. Developing conceptual models and using statistical analyses to identify associations among elements of the model is an important and necessary precursor to designing randomized controlled experiments to test the effects of specific curricular interventions on student learning outcomes. The study is methodologically innovative in its use of sophisticated statistical techniques to estimate the relative effects of different aspects of the curriculum on student learning outcomes and to compare these effects cross-nationally. The sophistication of the analysis is one reason that we chose to include this study as an example of recent work on causal modeling. In isolating the effects of different aspects of the curriculum on learning, the study suggests where curricular interventions might be most effective.

Study Design, Data, and Approach

TIMSS is an international comparative study of mathematics and science achievement involving nearly 50 countries.[53] TIMSS focused on three populations of students: (a) two adjacent grades consisting of the majority of 9-year-olds in each country; (b) two adjacent grades consisting of the majority of 13-year-olds in each country; and (c) all students in the last year of secondary school, with subpopulations focusing on those studying advanced mathematics, physics, or both. For each population, mathematics and science assessments were administered toward the end of the school year.[54] In addition, students completed surveys concerning their interests, study habits, motivations, and classroom experiences; surveys were also completed by teachers and school administrators.

Curriculum measures. To identify and measure curriculum standards and textbooks for students participating in TIMSS, the investigators systematically collected the official content standards (e.g., curriculum frameworks, guides, national curricula) and a representative sample of student textbooks from each participating country.[55] Documents were first divided into specific segments or units. For content standards, units specifying content and objectives were the most prevalent. For textbooks, lesson units (the amount of material likely to be covered in 1 to 3 days of instruction) were the most prevalent. Units were further divided into homogeneous blocks for purposes of coding.[56]

To measure teacher implementation (teacher coverage and instructional time), the investigators used responses to questions in the TIMSS Teacher Questionnaire, which was administered to teachers of students in the study. Teachers were asked the number of lessons devoted to specific topics of instruction. Topics were taken from the TIMSS mathematics and science frameworks. Listed topics covered all content areas in the frameworks and were tightly related to specific content topics. For each listed topic, teachers were also asked to indicate how much instructional time was devoted to the topic.[57]

Achievement measures. Scores on the TIMSS achievement tests were used to measure achievement gains in mathematics and science at specific grades. Because test items were based on content categories specified in the TIMSS mathematics and science frameworks, it was possible to identify the specific content being measured by particular test items.[58] Achievement gains ideally are measured at two time points for each individual student, so that learning growth can be assessed over time for each student. Due to the design of the TIMSS study, this was not possible. However, because the same tests were administered to two adjacent grades for 9- and 13-year-olds, it was possible to measure achievement at the end of both grades and to construct national estimates of the gains from one grade to the next.

Analyses and Results

To test their model of the relationships among aspects of the curriculum and student learning, the investigators estimated a structural model (one of several analytic approaches taken) that takes into account both the direct and indirect relationships of each of these aspects to student achievement gains, controlling for the other aspects of the curriculum. In cross-national comparisons that controlled for national wealth and other country-level variables, results for the estimated structural model of the effects of the four aspects of curriculum on student achievement gains provide general support for the investigators' conceptual model. For example, in mathematics, content standards were found to be related to teacher implementation both directly and indirectly through textbook coverage; teacher implementation was, in turn, related to achievement gains. In general, the more coverage of topics by a country (whether in content standards, textbooks, teacher coverage, or instructional time), the greater were student achievement gains for that country. These relationships, however, were not uniform across countries as countries varied in content coverage.

In science, a more complex pattern of relationships emerged. Content standards were directly related to student gains, as was teacher implementation (in terms of both instructional time and the percentage of teachers covering a topic). For these two measures of curriculum, the conclusions are essentially the same as for mathematics. The greater the priority a country assigned to a given topic in its content standards, the greater the achievement gains for that topic at eighth grade. The strength of this relationship depended on the country involved. In science, however, the relationship between textbook coverage and achievement gains was negative, indicating that the greater a country's textbook coverage of a topic (relative to other topics), the lower were the achievement gains for that topic.[59] In contrast to mathematics, there was no direct relationship between content standards and textbook coverage, nor was there a direct relationship between content standards and teacher instructional time. Overall, these results suggest that content standards were unrelated to textbook coverage in science.

Country-specific analyses were also conducted. For the United States, the investigators found that, for both mathematics and science, textbook coverage had a strong direct relationship to achievement gains, as well as a strong indirect relationship through instructional time allotted to particular topics. There was little variation in content standards within the United States because content standards covered virtually every mathematics and science topic included in the TIMSS assessments.

Hierarchical linear modeling was used to analyze the relationship between classroom instructional time and mathematics achievement across classrooms and schools within the United States; indicators of student SES and aggregate classroom SES were included in the model. The relationship of student SES to both achievement and opportunities to learn, as measured by instructional time and teacher coverage, has been documented in numerous studies in the United States and with multiple datasets (see, e.g., Anderson, Hollinger, & Conaty, 1993; Burstein, 1993; McKnight et al., 1987; Schmidt, McKnight, Cogan, Jakwerth, & Houang, 1999; Raudenbush, Fotiu, & Cheong, 1998; Stevenson, Schiller, & Schneider, 1994). Thus, in examining the relationship between achievement gains and aspects of the curriculum, it was necessary to adjust for student and classroom SES.[60]

Results of this analysis indicated that differences in achievement gains across eighth-grade classrooms were related to the amount of instructional time teachers allocated to particular topics, even when adjusting for differences across classrooms in SES and prior achievement. In general, the greater the instructional time devoted to a particular topic (measured as a percentage of total instructional time), the greater were achievement gains for that topic. The relationship between instructional time and mathematics achievement gains was positive and significant for all subtest areas in geometry, algebra, and proportionality. However, the relationship between achievement gains and instructional time devoted to whole numbers and fractions was negative and significant. These are topics typically taught in earlier grades, so instructional time devoted to these topics in eighth grade may do little to improve students' mastery of the topics.

Demanding performance expectations were also positively related to achievement gains for several advanced topics, including polygons and circles, three-dimensional geometry, and functions. These results suggest that engaging children in activities that go beyond routine drill and practice has an effect beyond the amount of time devoted to instruction. For U.S. eighth graders, the *quality* as well as the quantity of instruction appears to be important to achievement gains in mathematics, at least for these topics. Additional analyses examined predicted increases in achievement associated with increases in instructional time devoted to particular topics. The largest predicted increases were for geometry-related areas, proportionality problems, and equations; these were topics in which the United States generally did not provide much topic coverage. These results suggest that even a modest increase in the instructional time devoted to these topics could substantially increase student learning gains.

Implications for Estimating Causal Effects

The use of structural modeling allows the investigators to model the potential causal relationships between curriculum and learning. They are able to estimate both direct and indirect relationships between specific aspects of the curriculum and student achievement gains. For example, in mathematics, content standards appear to influence learning directly as well as indirectly through textbook coverage and teacher implementation. The investigators thus are able to identify variables through which learning may occur, information that is important in designing intervention studies.

Although this study does not provide evidence of a causal relationship between curriculum and learning, it does provide evidence of a strong association between them based on several different measures. In many cases, the aspects of the curriculum related to achievement gains differed for different topics and countries. However, some significant relationship between curriculum and achievement gains was found for all but five countries, even when controlling for national wealth and other country-level variables.

The investigators note several limitations of the study. They observe that "measures used in analyses are not perfect indicators of [curriculum] emphasis, neither do they function as perfect statistical indicators" (p. 359). In turn, measures of achievement gain are based on comparisons of the assessment scores of students from adjoining grades rather than on differences in the scores of the same students at two different time points (a longitudinal design). The investigators also acknowledge that both longitudinal studies and experiments with randomization are needed to refine their analysis of curricular effects.

Despite its limitations, this study moves us much closer to being able to construct and implement intervention studies designed to assess the causal relationship between curriculum and learning. The investigators' analysis of a large-scale observational dataset provides guidance on where to focus our efforts with respect to providing adequate coverage of topics as well as creating greater coherence across topics and aspects of the curriculum. For example, textbook coverage in the United States was found to have strong relationships to achievement gains in science and mathematics (both directly and indirectly through teacher instructional time), suggesting that increased textbook coverage of particular topics would result in achievement gains for those topics. The analysis of the relationship between instructional time and mathematics achievement among U.S. eighth graders also suggests that additional time devoted to particular topics in geometry and algebra would result in fairly large achievement gains for these topics. In addition, for certain advanced topics, the positive relationship between mathematics achievement and performance demands, as measured by the complexity of instructional activities students engaged in, points to the importance of the quality as well as the quantity of instruction for student learning. These findings suggest a potential focus for intervention studies based on experimental designs with randomization.

Case IV. A Standard Analytic Approach: "The Role of Gender and Friendship in Advanced Course-Taking"

In "The Role of Gender and Friendship in Advanced Course-Taking," Riegle-Crumb et al. (2006) examine the role of friendship groups in male and female high school students' advanced course-taking using data from the National Longitudinal Study of Adolescent Health. Given the continuing gender gap in science and mathematics achievement, the investigators are particularly interested in whether friends positively influence girls' advanced high school course-taking in these subjects. Focusing on the importance of same-sex friends as role models and sources of support, they examine whether girls who have high-achieving same-sex friends early in high school are more likely to enroll in advanced mathematics and science courses in their junior and senior years.

Research Questions and Theoretical Frame

Three research questions are addressed in the study: (a) Is same-sex friends' academic achievement positively associated with the advanced course-taking of male and female students? (b) Is same-sex friends' academic achievement more strongly associated with girls' advanced course-taking in mathematics and science (stereotypically male subject areas) than with their advanced course-taking in English (a stereotypically female subject area)? and (c) Do gender and friendship group composition interact such that there is a stronger relationship between same-sex friends' academic performance and girls' advanced course-taking when girls' friendship groups are predominantly female?

Theories of adolescent development suggest that peers become increasingly important during adolescence (see, e.g., Coleman, 1961; Erikson, 1968). By the time adolescents enter high school, they spend less time with their families and more time with friends. Depending on the nature of the relationship, friends may positively or negatively influence behavior. The social-psychological literature on adolescent development suggests that friendships may function differently for males and females. Girls' friendships with each other tend be more supportive and encouraging than friendships between boys

(Beutel & Marini, 1995; Felmlee, 1999; Giordano, 2003; McCarthy, Felmlee, & Haga, 2004; South & Haynie, 2004). Boys' friendships tend to be more competitive and activity-based, whereas girls' friendships are more cooperative and centered on discussion (Beutel & Marini, 1995). Although friendships with the opposite sex emerge in adolescence, same-sex friends continue to be important companions and role models and may have a greater influence on academic outcomes (Schneider & Stevenson, 1999).

Limitations of Previous Research on Peer Influences

Previous research on adolescent friendships has focused primarily on their potential to negatively influence behavior through encouraging drinking, drug use, or other problem behaviors (see, e.g., Granic & Dishion, 2003; Matsueda & Anderson, 1998; Warr, 1993; Weermand & Smeenk, 2005). The potential for friendships to positively influence adolescent behavior and development has received less attention. The few studies that have been done suggest that friends can play an important role in encouraging academic achievement (Crosnoe, Cavanaugh, & Elder, 2003; Epstein, 1983; Hallinan & Williams, 1990). Given the potential importance of friendships to educational outcomes, Riegle-Crumb et al. (2006) focus on whether having high-achieving friends of the same sex is associated with advanced course-taking, particularly in mathematics and science.

Although women have begun to enter mathematics and science occupations in greater numbers, and gender differences in mathematics and science test scores have declined over the past few decades, girls are still less likely to express interest in mathematics and science in high school or to see themselves as competent in these subjects, even when they perform at similar levels (Benbow & Minor, 1986; Correll, 2001; Xie & Shauman, 2003). Building on previous research indicating the importance of adult mentors and same-sex schools and class-rooms in promoting girls' interest and advanced course-taking in mathematics and science, Riegle-Crumb et al. (2006) suggest that girls whose same-sex friends are high achieving may be more likely to take advanced coursework in mathematics and science.[61] Such friends may help to establish norms about doing well in these subjects, function as role models, and serve as sources of emotional or psychological support. Riegle-Crumb and her colleagues, in turn, suggest that this association will be stronger in the context of a friendship group that is predominantly female.

Identifying Potential Causal Effects Using Conventional Statistical Techniques

Friends are not selected at random. It is therefore not possible to design a randomized experiment to investigate the potential effects of friendships on an outcome such as advanced course-taking. Approximating a randomized experiment through an approach such as propensity score matching is also not feasible. Propensity score matching assumes that there is a mechanism by which individuals are assigned to groups when assignment is nonrandom, as in the case of retention and promotion. Friends are not assigned, however; they are chosen, and many factors other than academic performance may influence that choice for any given individual. To examine the relationship of friendship characteristics to academic outcomes, analysts must rely on non-experimental designs and use statistical techniques to adjust for selection bias.

As Riegle-Crumb et al. (2006) indicate, selection bias is a primary concern in studies attempting to model friend-ship influences. Because individuals may select friends who have similar characteristics, it can be difficult to determine whether friends have an independent (socializing) effect on an individual's behavior. Although the investigators argue that friendship effects on course-taking are likely the result of both selection and socialization, they take several steps to reduce the likelihood that any given association is due only to selection. For example, in attempting to isolate the relationship between same-sex friends' grades and advanced course-taking in a given subject, they controlled for the influence of respondents' grades in the same year and course level in that subject. They also checked to determine whether students who were high achievers were more likely than low achievers to benefit from having high-achieving friends; no significant differences between high and low achievers were found in these analyses. In correlating respondents' grades with their same-sex friends' average grades for a given subject, they found only a moderate association ($r = .4$), suggesting that students selected their friends based on a number factors other than academic achievement.

Measuring advanced course-taking at a later time point (11th and 12th grades) than friends' academic achievement also reduced potential selection bias. By examining multiple outcomes (male and female advanced course-taking in math, science, and English), the investigators were also able determine whether relationships between friends' academic achievement and students' advanced course-taking varied by gender and subject. If associations vary across outcomes, then the likelihood that these results are due to selection bias rather than socialization is reduced.

Although there are statistical procedures for reducing bias, there is always the possibility that observed or unobserved characteristics associated with the outcome have been omitted from analytic models. It is therefore not possible to draw causal inferences from these analyses; they can only demonstrate associations between particular characteristics and outcomes of interest, and analysts should be careful not to use causal language in describing their results. However, well-designed observational analyses can provide insights into relationships that cannot be studied experimentally, provide evidence that confirms the results of previous studies, and suggest where interventions that can be studied experimentally might be most effective.

Study Design, Data, and Approach

To investigate the role of friends in students' advanced course-taking, the investigators used data from the National Longitudinal Study of Adolescent Health (Add Health) and the study's high school transcript data component. The Add Health Study included an In-School Survey, administered in the fall of 1994 to almost all students in Grades 7–12 in a nationally representative sample of schools, and three waves of In-Home Survey data collected from a representative sample of students in each school in 1995 (Wave I), 1996 (Wave II), and 2000–2001 (Wave III). In 2002–2003, high school transcript data were collected from the high schools attended by Wave III respondents.[62] For purposes of analyses, the investigators selected only students who were 9th and 10th graders in 1994–1995, had completed the In-School Survey and the Wave I In-Home Survey, and for whom high school transcript data were available. This selection process resulted in a subsample of approximately 2,500 students. The subsample is generalizable to U.S. 9th- and 10th-grade students with at least some friends who attended the same high school; statistical procedures were employed (weights) that make groups of individuals (categorized by race and ethnicity) in the subsample proportional to their numbers in the U.S. population.[63]

Measure of advanced course-taking. Advanced course-taking in science, mathematics, and English, the outcome measures in this analysis, were measured based on students' enrollment in their junior or senior year in high school in the following subjects: physics (science), pre-calculus or calculus (math), and advanced placement (AP) English or honors English IV (English), as recorded in the high school transcript file. These are the most advanced courses offered in each of these subject areas and typically are taken in the junior or senior year because of the prerequisites for course entry. Course information was coded using a classification scheme developed by the National Center for Education Statistics.

Friends' characteristics. The measures of friends' characteristics used to predict these outcomes were taken from students' responses to the In-School Survey. On the survey, students were asked to identify their five closest female friends and five closest male friends.[64] Measures of friends' academic performance include grades earned in science, mathematics, and English courses at the beginning of high school. Because prior research indicated that the academic performance of same-sex friends was more likely to influence girls' rather than boys' course-taking decisions, measures of the average grades of same-sex friends in each of these subjects were separately constructed for males and females. A dichotomous measure of the gender composition of students' friendship groups was also created.[65] To determine whether girls with predominantly high-achieving female friends were more likely to take advanced coursework, an interaction term was created by combining the average grades of same-sex friends in a given subject with the composition of the friendship group (i.e., predominantly female versus gender-equal or predominantly male).[66]

To gauge students' levels of involvement with friends, measures of activities that students engaged in with friends were constructed. On surveys, students indicated for each friend listed whether they had, in the past week, visited the friend's house, spent time together after school, talked on the phone, and/or spent time together over the weekend. Responses were summed for each friend and averaged across friends.[67]

Analyses and Results

The authors used logistic regression analysis to estimate the probability that students would enroll in physics, pre-calculus or calculus, and AP English or honors English IV in their junior or senior year of high school.[68] Separate analyses for males and females were conducted for each of these subjects.

For girls, having a predominantly female friendship group was not, by itself, associated with taking physics in the junior or senior year of high school. Grades of same-sex friends, however, were associated with an increased likelihood of taking physics. For example, as the science grades of a girl's female friends increased, the odds that the girl would take physics by the end of high school increased by a factor of approximately 1.5. There was also a significant positive effect for the interaction of friendship group composition (predominantly female) and grades of same-sex friends, indicating that the effect of same-sex friends' science grades was even stronger when girls' friendship groups were predominantly female. For girls, high parent expectations for college were also associated with an increased probability of taking physics.

In the model estimating the likelihood that girls would take calculus or pre-calculus by the end of high school, there was a significant overall association between friendship group composition and advanced course-taking (termed the main effect), such that girls with predominantly female friends were 1.7 times more likely to take calculus or pre-calculus as juniors or seniors. While there was a positive association between same-sex friends' mathematics grades and advanced course-taking, there was also a significant association for the interaction of friendship group composition with same-sex friends' average grades in mathematics early in high school. While all girls appeared to benefit from having girlfriends with higher math grades early in high school, those whose friendship group was predominantly female were the most likely to take advanced coursework in math by the end of high school.

In contrast to the results for the mathematics and science models, friendship group composition was not significantly associated with girls' advanced course-taking in English. Regardless of the gender composition of their friendship group, girls whose same-sex friends' earned higher grades in English at the beginning of high school (controlling on their own freshman-year English grades) were more likely to take AP or honors English by the end of high school. For example, as the English grades of a girl's female friends increased, the odds that the girl would take AP/honors English by the end of high school increased by a factor of approximately 1.9.

For male students, the grades of same-sex friends had no association with the likelihood of taking advanced coursework in any of the subjects considered. With respect to the gender composition of the friendship group, males whose friendship groups were predominantly male were actually less likely to take physics than those whose friendship groups were gender-equal or predominantly female.

Overall, these results indicate that the grades of same-sex friends are positively associated with the advanced course-taking of female students in all three subjects, but have no association with the advanced course-taking of males. In addition, the association of same-sex friends' grades and girls' advanced course-taking in mathematics and science is stronger when their friendship groups are predominantly female. To estimate the size of these effects, the investigators predicted the probabilities of taking physics, calculus/pre-calculus, or AP/honors English for a White female who did not have a predominantly female friendship group or had friends with a B average in each subject; the investigators then examined the change in probability when these conditions were altered. For physics, the investigators found that the probability of taking this course almost doubled when a girl's friends were mostly female and earned mostly A's in science. For calculus/pre-calculus, having predominantly female friends who earned mostly A's increased a girl's probability of taking the course from approximately .4 to .7.

Implications for Estimating Causal Effects

This is not a study that documents a causal relationship between friendship groups and student course-taking. It does show, through a longitudinal analysis of a large-scale, nationally representative dataset, some factors that are likely to increase the probability of taking advanced courses. The type of analysis used is representative in many ways of the majority of quantitative work being conducted in the field of education, but the study also has several strengths that make it a good example of this type of research. The investigators identify a research problem that cannot be studied experimentally. Relationships with peers and friends cannot readily be manipulated and studied in the context of an experiment. The investigators do not assume that they have discovered causal effects. At the same time, they are very aware of issues of selection bias and take several steps to reduce it as much as possible within the limits of their research question and dataset. Their work helps to identify one of the potential factors contributing to the gender gap in mathematics and science achievement. These results, combined with those of other studies, provide converging evidence on gender differences in course-taking patterns. Such results are persuasive in the absence of experimental designs.

The investigators also estimate the magnitude of the relationships of friends' grades and friendship group composition to advanced course-taking. In all cases, they find that same-sex friends' grades early in high school had a substantial association with girls' advanced course-taking. Such a finding is important in determining whether to develop an intervention that builds on the effects of friendship groups on advanced course-taking. An association between friends' grades and advanced course-taking could be statistically significant but still be negligible in terms of magnitude. In this instance, it would make no sense to design an intervention that attempted to promote friendships that were supportive of advanced course-taking. If these effects are large, however, it may be worthwhile to develop and evaluate an intervention designed to promote the formation of peer relationships that are supportive of girls' advanced course-taking in mathematics and science. Schneider and Stevenson (1999), for example, argue that student activity groups such as school-sponsored clubs are particularly important contexts for promoting the development of stable peer relationships around shared interests and activities. An activity-based group designed to encourage girls' interest in mathematics and science might be one context in which to promote peer relationships around such interests. If a goal is to develop an intervention intended to reduce the gender gap in these subjects, it is critical to identify a context in which such an intervention might be introduced.

Chapter 4 Notes

33 Secondary analyses are analyses of existing datasets.

34 Details of the Tennessee Class Size Experiment and results of the study have been presented in a number of publications, including Achilles, Finn, and Bain (1997), Finn and Achilles (1990, 1999), Kreuger (1999), and Nye et al. (2000).

35 This subset of schools ranged from 71% (in Grade 1) to 78% (in Grades 2 and 3) of the schools in the complete sample. A comparison of demographic characteristics of the schools in the analytic sample with those in the complete sample revealed that these characteristics were similar for the two samples.

36 Reading and mathematics test scores from the Stanford Achievement Test (SAT), administered at the end of each school year in kindergarten through third grade, served as the measures of student achievement. In analyses of achievement gains, student achievement scores from the prior year were included in the models. Within-classroom variables included student gender, SES (coded as 1 if a student received a free or reduced-price lunch, otherwise coded as 0), and minority group status (coded as 1 if a student was Black, Hispanic, or Asian, and coded as 0 if the student was White). Between-classroom variables included class size and presence of an instructional aide, teacher experience, and teacher education.

37 Previous studies also confirmed that these deviations did not bias results (see Krueger, 1999; Nye et al., 2000).

38 However, students and teachers were not randomly assigned to schools. As Nye et al. (2000) note, "It is clear [from observational studies] that teachers are not randomly allocated to schools. Research on teacher allocation to schools has documented that schools with high proportions of low-income and minority students often have difficulty recruiting and retaining high-quality teachers" (p. 249). See results reported by Darling-Hammond (1995), Krei (1998), and Langford, Loeb, and Wyckoff (2002). By including school characteristics in their model, Nye et al. were able to investigate whether teacher effects varied systematically across schools.

39 In order to decompose the variation between students, classrooms, and schools, a three-level model was used (students, classrooms, and schools).

40 Teacher effects on reading and mathematics achievement were approximately twice as large as school effects at Grade 2 and approximately three times as large as school effects at Grade 3.

41 In Grades 1–3, teacher effects on mathematics achievement were nearly twice as large as teacher effects on reading achievement.

42 Between-school variation in achievement status (each year and at third grade) was larger than the between-school variation in achievement gains, suggesting that teacher effects are closer in magnitude to school effects for achievement status. In other words, teachers have a greater impact than schools on student achievement gains from one year to the next. With respect to students' overall achievement (each year and at the end of third grade), however, teacher and school effects are similar in magnitude. Note that school effects are associational, not causal, because students and teachers were not randomly assigned to schools in the experiment.

43 Across grades, the proportion of the total variance in reading achievement accounted for by teacher effects was 1.4 to 1.7 times higher in low- versus high-SES schools; the proportion of the total variance in mathematics achievement accounted for by teacher effects was 1.6 to 3.7 times higher in low- versus high-SES schools.

44 Because large-scale datasets generally include comprehensive background information on large numbers of students (e.g., gender, race/ethnicity, family structure, SES, prior academic achievement, and a host of other variables), a large number of characteristics can be taken into account in computing propensity scores. Such large-scale longitudinal datasets also include data on students' performance on standardized tests over time, making it possible to examine differences in cognitive growth of retained and promoted students who are at similar risk of retention.

45 Hong and Raudenbush compared the 11,843 students in their analytic sample with the full ECLS sample to determine whether the analytic sample was a representative subsample. They did find some differences. The analytic sample had a lower percentage of poor and minority children (a 2–3% difference) and were less likely to come from non-English-speaking families (a 4% difference).

46 For a random sample of 4,024 students, assessment data were also obtained in the fall of the treatment year.

47 Classroom and school characteristics were also significant predictors of retention. Students who were in kindergarten classes with higher proportions of boys, higher proportions of younger children (e.g., 4-year-olds), and higher proportions of children who were repeating kindergarten were more likely to be retained. Teachers of such kindergarten classes also reported more behavioral problems at the beginning of the year and tended to spend less time in reading and literacy instruction and to cover lower-level content in reading and mathematics. Children were also more likely to be retained if they attended schools that were smaller in size, nonpublic, had inadequate instructional resources and facilities, lower teacher salaries, and fewer classroom teachers and ESL teachers.

48 For both reading and math, the investigators found that the *observed* achievement gap between retained and promoted students doubled in width between the fall and spring of the treatment year. On the basis of estimated growth rates, if retained students had instead been promoted, their growth rates would have been comparable to those of promoted students, substantially reducing the achievement gap in both reading and math.

49 Results of supplementary analyses also suggested that there was a diminishing effect of retention for students who had a greater probability of being retained. In other words, if these high-risk students had instead been promoted, their growth trajectories would have remained low. However, the authors indicate that "even for those who tended to be diagnosed as in a relatively higher need of repeating a grade, there was no evidence that they received any immediate benefit from the retention treatment. In general, kindergarten retention seemed to have constrained the learning potential of all but the highest-risk children" (Hong & Raudenbush, 2005, p. 220).

50 It was assumed that there might be unmeasured student- and school-level characteristics that were comparable to the most important student- and school-level variables in their models for each subject area. Adjustments for the inclusion of these hypothetical variables were made, and retention effects were re-estimated (Lin, Psaty, & Kronmal, 1998; Rosenbaum & Rubin, 1983; Rosenbaum, 1986, 2002).

51 In their examination of the characteristics of retention and nonretention schools, the investigators identified 238 school-level variables that were associated with retention. They found that nonpublic schools, suburban schools, and schools with lower percentages of minority students and teachers were more likely to adopt a kindergarten retention policy. In general, retention schools tended to have smaller class sizes, greater parent involvement, and fewer disciplinary problems than nonretention schools. In the pretreatment year, kindergartners in retention schools also had higher average reading scores than those in nonretention schools. However, when propensity score methods were used to create groups that were balanced with respect to these school characteristics, no significant differences in the learning outcomes of students were found between groups.

52 Structural modeling (also referred to as structural equation modeling, or SEM) is an extension of regression analysis that offers several advantages. In contrast to multivariate regression analysis—where associations between multiple predictor variables and one outcome variable are modeled, and associations among predictor variables are adjusted for—structural modeling allows for the inclusion of more than one outcome variable. Whereas in multivariate regression analysis a variable can be *either* a predictor variable or an outcome variable but not both, in structural modeling a given variable may be an outcome variable with respect to some variables and a predictor of other variables. For example, teacher instructional practices may be an outcome of content standards and textbook coverage but may also be a predictor, along with content standards and textbook coverage, of student achievement; structural modeling allows the analyst to model this complex relationship.

Although structural modeling is sometimes referred to as causal modeling, it does not allow the analyst to make causal inferences. As Norman and Streiner (2004) observe, "Cause and effect can be established only through the proper research design [e.g., a randomized controlled experiment]" (p. 159). Structural modeling is a model-testing procedure. A conceptual model that specifies relationships among a set of variables is tested by means of appropriate statistical procedures.

53 When this study was conducted, the name was as it appears in the text. The name has now been changed to Trends in International Mathematics and Science Study.

54 The items included in the TIMSS assessments are based on a categorization of topics that describe possible contents of the mathematics and science curricula in participating countries and the performance that might be expected of students with respect to these content areas. As the authors note, these category systems—the TIMSS mathematics and science frameworks—"were developed to provide a common language for describing and examining what students in many different countries study in their schools. Although the frameworks were developed and published in English, they needed to be sufficiently broad to include any topic found in any of the participating countries' curricula, yet sufficiently precise as to provide accurate portraits that could be compared and analyzed" (p. 21). Because a major focus of TIMSS was on 9- and 13-year-olds, the curriculum frameworks were developed with elementary and middle school students in mind. In addition to specifying subject matter topics, the TIMSS frameworks also specify performance expectations ("what students were expected to do with particular subject matter topics") and perspectives ("any overarching orientation to the subject matter and its place in the disciplines and in the everyday world") (p. 363).

55 The authors note that "the selection criteria for the documents that would be coded—standards and textbooks—required that a national sample include sufficient documents that pertained to at least 50 percent of the students in the TIMSS focal grades. In addition a country's document sample was required to cover all major regions and all types of schools and educational tracks (e.g., public, private, vocational, technical, and academic)" (p. 24).

56 "Each block [from the TIMSS mathematics and science frameworks] . . . was coded by assigning as many content categories, performance expectations, and perspectives to it as were needed to characterize the content" (p. 24). The measures of standards and textbooks were for a specific year of schooling (i.e., fourth grade or eighth grade). The measures of classroom instruction were based on teachers' responses regarding topic coverage in a particular class during the year in which the TIMSS achievement tests were administered.

57 Instructional time was coded as follows: 1–5 periods/lessons; 6–10 periods/lessons; 11–15 periods/lessons; or more than 15 periods/lessons.

58 The validity of the TIMSS test items was assessed by several panels of U.S. mathematicians and scientists. Panel members concluded that the items included in the TIMSS assessments adequately represented and measured the specific topics covered. Measures of reliability (an indication of the amount of measurement error in the tests) indicated that measurement error was relatively low. The median reliability estimates for the TIMSS eighth-grade mathematics and sciences tests were .78 and .89, respectively (coefficients range from 0 to 1.00; higher coefficients indicate greater reliability/lower measurement error).

59 Additional analyses were conducted to determine why there was a negative relationship between textbook coverage and achievement gains in science. The analyses revealed that three content areas primarily accounted for this relationship: energy and physical processes, chemical changes, and structure of matter. Both physical processes and chemical changes constituted a large proportion of textbook coverage across countries relative to other topics, but student gains for these topics were only average. In contrast, the topic of structure of matter constituted a small proportion of textbook coverage but showed the largest achievement gains. When these topics were dropped from the analysis, the relationship between textbook coverage and student achievement gains was much less negative. One explanation for these anomalous findings may be that the TIMSS test produced floor and ceiling effects for these topics in seventh grade, which limited estimates of achievement gains between seventh and eighth grades.

60 Due to sampling limitations, it was not possible to relate classroom instructional time to student achievement gains in science. Many countries organized eighth-grade science instruction into separate courses, and sampling may have included teachers of different science courses within a given country, making it difficult to link student and science teacher data. This set of analyses therefore focuses only on mathematics.

61 See, e.g., Baker and Leary (1995), Dryler (1998), Eccles, Jacobs, and Harold (1990), Lee (2002), Shu and Marini (1998), Seymour and Hewitt (1997), and Stake and Nicken (2005) on the importance of adult mentors. See Burkham, Lee, and Smerdon (1997), Shapka and Keating (2003), and Lee and Bryk (1986) on student interest and course-taking in science and mathematics in predominantly female environments.

62 Overall, data were collected from six nationally representative cohorts of students based on their grade level (7th through 12th) in 1994–1995.

63 In addition to weights, the analysts used a statistical program to account for the clustering of students within a school when calculating standard errors, that is, an estimate of the deviation of the sample mean from the population mean.

64 Since almost all students within a given school were surveyed, the investigators were to able link the survey responses of identified friends with those of the respondent. Measures of friends' characteristics were thus based on the friends' self-reports rather than on respondents' characterizations of their friends' qualities.

65 A friendship group that had a greater number of same-sex friends was coded as 1; a group that had a greater number of opposite-sex friends or was gender-equitable was coded as 0.

66 An interaction term is a variable that takes into account the associations between two measures in order to predict their relationship with the dependent variable, independent of the separate effects of each.

67 All models included the following variables: students' race and ethnicity; parents' education level; family income; family structure; a measure of students' self-perceived intelligence relative to peers; students' educational expectations; parental expectations; school engagement; school attachment; students' freshman year course placements in science, math, and English; and their corresponding grades in those subjects. Freshman-year math and science course placements were assigned a numerical coding based on the level of the course taken (e.g., for science, no science = 0; remedial science = 1; general/earth science = 2; biology I = 3). For English, a dichotomous measure was created indicating whether the student was enrolled in an honors English course as a freshman.

68 Several types of analysis are used to identify associations between the dependent and independent variables; the specific approach used depends on the nature of the outcome variable being analyzed and how it is measured. In its most easily interpretable form, this procedure is termed *linear regression* and is used to test whether there is a linear relationship between an outcome variable and a set of variables believed to be associated with that outcome; the strength of relationship between the dependent variable and each of the independent variables is also calculated, adjusting for any associations that might exist among the set of independent variables. When an outcome variable is a continuous variable such as grade point average (GPA, which can take on a range of values, usually between 0 and 4), the strength of this relationship can be described in terms of the change in the outcome variable (e.g., an increase or decrease in GPA) associated with the change in a particular independent variable (e.g., hours per week spent on homework). Say, for example, an increase of an hour per week in study time is found to be associated with an increase of 0.25 in students' overall GPA (controlling for other variables included in the analysis).

When the outcome measure is dichotomous (coded 0 or 1), as is the case in this study, the outcome either occurs or does not (e.g., a student either takes physics or does not). The outcome variable does not take on a range of values, as in the example above, but has only two values. The relationship between the dependent variable and an independent variable (e.g., friends' grades in science early in high school) cannot be meaningfully expressed as an increase or decrease in physics course-taking associated with friends' grades; what is being measured is not the number of physics courses taken but only whether the student did or did not take physics. In this case, it is desirable to express this relationship as the probability that the outcome will occur (taking physics) when certain conditions apply (e.g., friends earn higher or lower grades in science early in high school). This is done using a form of regression analysis known as logistic regression—the statistical technique used in this study.

In addition to the statistical analyses reported here, Riegle-Crumb et al. also conducted analyses using HLM, which allowed them to examine the variability in advanced course-taking both within and across schools. These analyses yielded similar results with respect to the associations between friendship groups and advanced course-taking regardless of the size of the sample within each school.

5. Conclusions and Recommendations

THERE IS A GENERAL CONSENSUS in the education research community on the need to increase the capacity of researchers to study educational problems scientifically. This report considers key issues involved in selecting research designs that allow investigators to draw valid causal inferences about treatment effects using large-scale observational datasets. It addresses why issues of establishing causal inference are of particular interest to education researchers, provides a brief explanation of how causality is commonly defined in the literature, and describes some of the tools that analysts use to approximate randomized experiments with observational data. The report also reviews four studies funded by NSF that illustrate the difficulties of and possibilities for making causal inferences when conducting studies focused on significant educational issues. These studies and other examples provided in this report are intended to help researchers and policymakers understand the strengths and weaknesses of various research designs and methods.[69]

Government funding agencies in the United States and elsewhere are at a critical juncture as they seek to determine what types of research studies to fund in an era of declining resources. At the same time, such agencies are faced with educational problems that have thus far proved intractable, such as closing the achievement gap between racial and ethnic groups with varying economic and social resources. As NSF, IES, and other government agencies review their portfolios and decide where they need to allocate scarce resources, we make the following suggestions.

Forming an Evidential Base With Observational Designs

National longitudinal datasets such as ECLS and the National Education Longitudinal Study of 1988–2000, designed and administered by NCES, are extremely useful sources of data for investigating educational problems and formulating policies. These datasets, constructed with stratified random samples based on population estimates, provide some of the most robust indicators of how students are performing academically and allow for exploratory analyses regarding why some children are more successful in school than others. The large samples on which these studies are based facilitate comparisons across various subgroups using measures such as age, gender, race/ethnicity, and social and economic resources. These datasets are widely accessible to researchers, enhancing capacity for replicating and extending findings to specific populations and settings. An additional benefit of these datasets is that they can be linked to other national datasets, including census information, facilitating the examination of neighborhood effects on achievement, school access, and resource inequities. Research based on these datasets has had a significant impact on our understanding of teacher effects on instruction, classroom resources that positively affect student learning, factors associated with dropout rates, high school graduation rates, postsecondary matriculation, and relationships between school organizations (sector effects, charter schools, and magnet schools) and student achievement. Secondary analyses of educational datasets, particularly those that contain information from students, parents, and teachers within institutions over time, continue to serve as one of the richest sources for evidence-based educational policy evaluation.[70]

Through statistical techniques, large-scale datasets can approximate some of the probable causes and effects that experiments can establish more conclusively. Analyses of large-scale datasets are particularly valuable when experiments are impossible or impractical, such as when examining the effect of corporal punishment on student learning. However, even with these data, which arguably are among the best we have, the findings have not consistently yielded information that could substantially improve our schools and change the educational opportunities of students, especially those who attend high-poverty schools and whose families have limited economic and social resources.

Certainly, these large-scale datasets could be more useful if the design and instruments were determined by some of the leading experts in the field. Often the design and instruments of longitudinal and other national large-scale studies are determined by precedent or produced within a short period so that careful review, discussion, and consideration of possible innovation are less likely to occur. In the instance of assessing effective accountability measures as identified in NCLB, a multipurpose longitudinal study could be conducted by embedding controlled field trials within a conventional stratified random sample of school districts that included an oversample of low-performing school districts.

In this report, we have highlighted how, with appropriate methods, observational datasets can be used to approximate randomized assignment to treatment and control conditions. Large-scale datasets have been somewhat underutilized for this purpose, and we encourage NSF, IES, and other funding agencies to promote studies that continue to explore and develop methodologies for approximating randomized experiments, support work that is designed to undertake such analyses, and recognize the importance of these studies for testing hypotheses, designing subsequent experiments, and measuring contextual effects.

There are tradeoffs between experiments and analyses of observational data. Kish (1987) observed that what makes an experiment especially powerful is that the conditions are tightly controlled. Well-designed experiments maximize internal validity, whereas nationally representative observational datasets maximize external validity (Campbell & Stanley, 1963). Both are important. As Hedges recently commented, randomized controlled trials are particularly efficient in measuring main effects (Hedges, 2004). However, analyses of observational datasets may be beneficial for estimating contextual conditions such as classroom composition or school organizational practices that may be indirectly influencing the effect of a specific intervention.

Education research is facing new challenges and opportunities due to the confluence of high expectations and new methodologies and datasets. It is important to underscore that the types of research questions addressed by education research projects should be of first concern and that appropriate methods should be employed to answer these questions more definitively. Researchers should be encouraged to investigate questions that deliberately test theories of practice and to obtain empirical data to examine rival explanations for behavior. To do so requires developing a portfolio that tests specific hypotheses about educational practice, tailors research questions to address the effects of programs and practices on specific populations, and, most important, derives frameworks and theoretical approaches that address questions of causal effects and the multiple methods that can be used to examine such questions.

Assessing the Relative Strengths of Experimental and Quasi-Experimental Designs

In deciding which proposals best address the research questions of interest to a funding agency, it is important to develop decision rules for evaluating the quality of proposed research. Below, we identify several criteria for evaluating the appropriateness and strengths of various research designs for investigating the effects of particular interventions.

Are randomized controlled trials a feasible design for addressing the research question(s)? If not, can treatment and control groups be identified using existing large-scale observational datasets? If so,

- How reliable are the measures?

- Does the research design include identification of possible causal mechanisms?

- Does the design specify the investigation of treatment effects for different populations of students?

- Does the design allow investigators to take into account the nested quality of educational settings? For example, are treatment effects examined at various levels of the educational system (e.g., classroom, school, and school district)?

- Has the researcher proposed an appropriate quasi-experimental design, such as propensity score matching?

The What Works Clearinghouse has developed a set of decision rules that can be used to assess the strength of quasi-experimental designs. These include criteria for classifying experimental and quasi-experimental research designs and for determining the strength of various designs with respect to drawing valid causal inferences. Other important characteristics of studies that should be evaluated are also identified, including (a) intervention fidelity; (b) outcome measures;

(c) the extent to which relevant people, settings, and measures are included in the study; (d) the extent to which the study allows for testing of the intervention's effect within subgroups; (e) statistical analysis; and (f) statistical reporting (see What Works Clearinghouse, http://www.whatworks.ed.gov).

If a randomized experiment cannot be approximated using a rigorous method such as propensity score matching, can an alternative method, such as a regression discontinuity design, a fixed effects model, or an instrumental variable approach, be used? If so,

- For a regression discontinuity design, can the investigators indicate how they will establish whether individuals just above and below the cutoff point for program entry have similar characteristics and probabilities of being accepted into the program? For example, are appropriate matching procedures proposed?

- If a fixed effects approach is proposed, do the investigators provide a clear rationale for treating a variable or variables as fixed, or time-invariant?

- If an instrumental variable is used, do the investigators provide a clear rationale for its selection?

- Do the investigators propose appropriate statistical techniques for comparing treatment group outcomes, fixing effects, or correctly implementing the instrumental variable?

- If a regression discontinuity design, fixed effects model, or instrumental variable approach cannot be used, what methods are proposed for correcting for selection bias and controlling for potentially confounding variables? Have the investigators clearly indicated the strengths and limitations of these methods?

In some cases it may be possible to use both experimental and quasi-experimental designs to address a particular research question. In such cases, funding agencies need to assess the relative strengths and weaknesses of the proposed designs with respect to (a) their potential for producing unbiased estimates of treatment effects, (b) possible difficulties that might arise in implementing the designs, and (c) the cost of each type of study.

If the design is experimental,

- Can investigators recruit a sufficient number of participants (e.g., school districts, schools, teachers, and students) to conduct the study?

- Can the study be implemented with fidelity? Are steps proposed for monitoring implementation to identify problems that may arise in designing and fielding the study (e.g., unsuccessful randomization, insufficient sample sizes for detecting treatment effects, movement of students between treatment and control conditions when individuals are randomized to treatment and control conditions, and differential attrition)?

If the design is quasi-experimental and propensity score methods are used,

- Are available measures comprehensive enough to create an aggregate variable for purposes of computing propensity scores?

- Is there sufficient overlap in the pretreatment characteristics of the treatment and control groups to warrant further analyses?

- Can students in the treatment and control groups be matched with respect to pretreatment characteristics so as to create equivalence in pretreatment characteristics within propensity score strata?

• Is the analytic sample large enough to detect treatment effects?

If both experimental and quasi-experimental designs are feasible and potential problems in implementation can be adequately addressed, then the decision regarding which design to implement may depend on the cost of each study. In the case of large-scale RCTs, these costs can be considerable. A well-designed quasi-experimental study using an existing large-scale national longitudinal dataset would generally be much less costly to implement. Using a quasi-experimental design does not preclude following it with a more tightly controlled experiment (i.e., it is not necessary to choose one or the other).

If existing observational datasets do not contain sufficient information for conducting a well-designed quasi-experiment, then funders should consider developing a study that builds on the strengths of both designs. For example, it may be possible to embed a multi-site randomized controlled trial within a large-scale longitudinal study based on a nationally representative sample of students, teachers, and schools, with an oversampling of low-income and minority students, or other groups most likely to benefit from a particular intervention.

Sustaining a Program of Evidential Research

In the past, NSF and other governmental agencies and private foundations have funded few randomized controlled trials in education. The enactment of the No Child Left Behind Act, in conjunction with other evidence-based movements internationally, raised awareness of the importance of conducting RCTs, particularly in education (Schneider, Kertcher, &

Offer, 2006). The importance of RCTs is clear, and it seems important that NSF and government agencies that fund education research develop and support a coherent and sustained program of experimentation to complement qualitative data on best practices such as interviews and classroom observations and descriptive and quantitative data on teacher quality, instructional practices, and student and teacher characteristics obtained from large-scale observational studies such as ECLS.

As the NRC's Committee on Scientific Research on Education makes clear in *Scientific Research in Education* (2002), the question of causal effects is but one of three general questions that drive research. This report has focused on how to establish that there is an effect (i.e., "Is there a systematic effect?"). What has been less emphasized are the two other question identified by the NRC: (1) "What is happening?" (i.e., what is occurring in a particular context, usually documented through thick description); and (2) "Why or how is it happening?" (i.e., What mechanisms are producing the effect that is observed?). These two questions are central to the design of experiments and their usefulness. They are also important for developing theories of cognition, learning, and social and emotional development. A program of evaluation built on a solid foundation of closely linked research using a variety of methods is needed to establish the basis for reliable and enduring knowledge about the effects of educational innovations.

The recent review of NSF's portfolio of mathematics projects provides a window into the research priorities of a specific program within a federal funding agency. This report concluded that NSF-funded projects in this area tend to focus on designing and implementing new interventions, tools, and methods, but are much less likely to address basic problems of teaching and learning or to synthesize results and identify new questions (NSF, 2004). Although NSF projects that focus on the design and implementation of new interventions or methods often include an evaluation component, project quality or effectiveness seldom has been evaluated using rigorous experimental and quasi-experimental designs. The challenge for funding agencies such as NSF is to develop a culture of both development and evaluation—one that attends to all points of the cycle of discovery, innovation, and application. In this report we recommend that researchers be required to discuss more directly their hypotheses and models of educational practice. Proposed research programs should answer questions about what mechanisms are important and how practitioners can apply the results of research or evaluation.

Considerable resources are currently available to help funding agencies and researchers evaluate the strengths of different study designs and to develop better-designed experiments and quasi-experiments. We have attempted to add to these resources by providing decision rules specific to the evaluation of studies based on large-scale, nationally representative datasets. Although embedding RCTs within future national longitudinal studies would strengthen the design of such studies, existing large-scale datasets remain a rich resource for descriptive statistics on nationally representative samples of students and subgroups (e.g., low-income and minority students); for identifying potential causal effects and mechanisms; and for providing valid evidence of causal effects through the use of rigorously designed quasi-experiments. These datasets have been underutilized for purposes of study replication. Properly analyzed, they present cost-effective alternatives for addressing causal questions about the effectiveness of educational interventions. The methods described for approximating randomized controlled experiments underscore the value of these datasets for generating and informing educational policy and practice.

Chapter 5 Notes

69 This report is not intended to be a "how to" manual for designing research studies or analyzing experimental or observational data. A number of resources are currently available for helping education researchers develop and implement well-designed randomized controlled experiments or quasi-experiments. We would recommend that Shadish, Cook, and Campbell (2002) be one of the first sources consulted.

70 Although most of the national datasets are unusually broad in scope, analytic limitations exist even among datasets that have hundreds of variables, many of which can be triangulated across different respondents. Common problems that researchers encounter with these datasets are missing data. Fortunately, researchers now have sophisticated techniques for imputing missing data (see, e.g., King, Honaker, Joseph, and Scheve, 2001, and Little and Rubin, 2002, on multiple imputation techniques). Similarly, Institutional Review Boards and government agencies are finding ways to secure confidentiality so that researchers can now link different datasets or create equating assessment protocols that allow them to identify and use similar variables across local, state, and national datasets.

References

Achilles, C. M., Finn, J. D., & Bain, H. P. (1997). Using class size to reduce the equity gap. *Education Leadership, 55*(4), 40–43.

Anderson, J., Hollinger, D., & Conaty, J. (1993). Re-examining the relationship between school poverty and student achievement. *ERS Spectrum, 11*(2), 21–31.

Angrist, J. D., Imbens, G. W., & Rubin, D. B. (1996). Identification of causal effects using instrumental variables (with commentary). *Journal of the American Statistical Association, 91*, 444–472.

Angrist, J. D., & Krueger, A. B. (1991). Does compulsory school attendance affect schooling and earnings? *Quarterly Journal of Economics, 106*(4), 979–1014.

Angrist, J. D., & Krueger, A. B. (1995). Split-sample instrumental variables estimates of the returns to schooling. *Journal of Business and Economic Statistics, 13*(2), 225–235.

Angrist, J. D., & Krueger, A. B. (2001). Instrumental variables and the search for identification: From supply and demand to natural experiments. *Journal of Economic Perspectives, 15*(4), 69–85.

Angrist, J. D., & Lavy, V. (1999). Using Maimonides' rule to estimate the effects of class size on academic achievement. *Quarterly Journal of Economics, 114*(2), 533–576.

Baker, D., & Leary, R. (1995). Letting girls speak out about science. *Journal of Research in Science Teaching, 32,* 3–7.

Barnow, B., Cain, G., & Goldberger, A. (1980). Issues in the analysis of selectivity bias. In E. Stromsdorfer & G. Farkas (Eds.), *Evaluation studies* (Vol. 5, pp. 43–59). Beverly Hills, CA: Sage.

Benbow, C., & Minor, L. (1986). Mathematically talented males and females and achievement in the high school sciences. *American Educational Research Journal, 23,* 425–439.

Beutel, A. M., & Marini, M. M. (1995). Gender and values. *American Sociological Review, 60*(3), 436–448.

Bidwell, C. (1965). The school as a formal organization. In J. G. March (Ed.), *Handbook of organizations* (pp. 972–1022). Chicago: Rand McNally.

Bidwell, C. (2000). School as context and construction: A social psychological approach to the study of schooling. In M. T. Hallinan (Ed.), *Handbook of the sociology of education* (pp. 13–37). New York: Kluwer Academic/Plenum.

Bidwell, C., Frank, K. A., & Quiroz, P. (1997). Teacher types, workplace controls, and the organization of schools. *Sociology of Education, 70*(4), 285–307.

Bifulco, R., & Ladd, H. F. (2006). The impacts of charter schools on student achievement: Evidence from North Carolina. *Education Finance and Policy, 1*(1), 50–99.

Bloch, M. (2004). A discourse that disciplines, governs, and regulates: The National Research Council's report on scientific research in education. *Qualitative Inquiry, 10*(1), 96–110.

Bloom, H. S. (1984). Accounting for no-shows in experimental evaluation designs. *Evaluation Review, 8,* 225–246.

Bound, J., Jaeger, D. A., & Baker, R. M. (1995). Problems with instrumental variables estimation when the correlation between the instruments and the exogenous explanatory variable is weak. *Journal of the American Statistical Association, 90,* 443–450.

Bryk, A. S., Lee, V. E., & Holland, P. B. (1993). *Catholic schools and the common good.* Cambridge, MA: Harvard University Press.

Bryk, A. S., & Raudenbush, S. W. (2002). *Hierarchical linear models* (2nd ed.). Thousand Oaks, CA: Sage Publications.

Burkham, D., Lee, V., & Smerdon, B. (1997). Gender and science learning early in high school: Subject matter and laboratory experiences. *American Educational Research Journal, 34,* 297–332.

Burstein, L. (Ed.). (1993). *The IEA study of mathematics III: Student growth and classroom processes* (Vol. 3). Oxford, UK: Pergamon Press.

Byrnes, D. A. (1989). Attitudes of students, parents, and educators toward repeating a grade. In L. A. Shepard & M. L. Smith (Eds.), *Flunking grades: Research and policies on retention* (pp. 108–131). Philadelphia: Falmer Press.

Campbell, D. T. (1969). Reforms as experiments. *American Psychologist, 25,* 409–429.

Campbell, D. T., & Stanley, J. C. (1963). Experimental and quasi-experimental designs for research on teaching. In N. L. Gage (Ed.), *Handbook of research on teaching.* Chicago: Rand McNally.

Cochran, W. G., & Cox, G. M. (1950). *Experimental design* (2nd ed.). New York: Wiley.

Cohen, J. (1988). *Statistical power analysis for the behavioral sciences* (2nd ed.). Hillsdale, NJ: Lawrence Erlbaum.

Coleman, J. (1961). *The adolescent society.* New York: Free Press.

Coleman, J., & Hoffer, T. (1987). *Public and private high schools: The impact of communities.* New York: Basic Books.

Cook, T. D. (2002). Randomized experiments in educational policy research: A critical examination of the reasons the educational evaluation community has offered for not doing them. *Educational Evaluation and Policy Analysis, 24*(3), 175–199.

Cook, T. D. (2007). Randomized experiments in education: Assessing the objections to doing them. *Economics of Innovation and New Technology, 16*(2), 31–49.

Cook, T. D. (in press). "Waiting for life to arrive": A history of the regression-discontinuity design in psychology, statistics and economics. *Journal of Econometrics.*

Correll, S. (2001). Gender and the career choice process: The role of biased self-assessments. *American Journal of Sociology, 106,* 1697–1730.

Cox, D. R. (1958a). *Planning of experiments.* New York: Wiley.

Cox, D. R. (1958b). The interpretation of the effects of non-additivity in the Latin square. *Biometrika, 45,* 69–73.

Crosnoe, R., Cavanagh, S., & Elder Jr., G. H. (2003). Adolescent friendships as academic resources: The intersection of friendship, race, and school disadvantage. *Sociological Perspectives, 46,* 331–352.

Cuddeback, G., Wilson, E., Orme, J. G., & Combs-Orme, T. (2004). Detecting and correcting sample selection bias. *Journal of Social Service Research, 30*(3), 19–33.

Cuijpers, P. (2003). Examining the effects of prevention programs on the incidence of new cases of mental disorders: The lack of statistical power. *American Journal of Psychiatry, 160*(8), 1385–1391.

Currie, J. (2003, June). *When do we really know what we think we know? Determining causality.* Invited paper presented at Work, Family, Health and Well-Being conference, NICHD Administration for Children and Families, Washington, DC.

Currie, J., & Thomas, D. (1995). Does Head Start make a difference? *American Economic Review, 85,* 341–364.

Currie, J., & Thomas, D. (1999). Does Head Start help Hispanic children? *Journal of Public Economics, 74,* 235–262.

Darling-Hammond, L. (1995). Inequality and access to knowledge. In J. A. Banks (Ed.), *The handbook of research on multicultural education* (pp. 465–483). New York: Macmillan.

Dignam, J. (2003, November). *From efficacy to effectiveness: Translating randomized controlled trial findings into treatment standards.* Paper presented at the invitational conference Conceptualizing Scale-Up: Multidisciplinary Perspectives, Data Research and Development Center, Washington, DC.

Dreeben, R., & Gamoran, A. (1986). Race, instruction, and learning. *American Sociological Review, 51*(5), 660–669.

Dryler, H. (1998). Parental role models, gender, and educational choice. *British Journal of Sociology, 49,* 375–398.

Eccles, J., Jacobs, J., & Harold, R. (1990). Gender role stereotypes, expectancy effects, and parents' socialization of gender differences. *Journal of Social Issues, 46,* 183–202.

Education Sciences Reform Act of 2002, Pub. L. No. 107-279. Retrieved September 3, 2004, from http://www.ed.gov/legislation/EdSciencesRef/

Eisenhart, M., & Towne, L. (2003). Contestation and change in national policy on scientifically based research. *Educational Researcher, 32*(7), 3138.

Epstein, J. L. (1983). The influence of friends on achievement and affective outcomes. In J. L. Epstein & N. Karweit (Eds.), *Friends in school: Patterns of selection and influence in secondary schools* (pp. 177–200). New York: Academic Press.

Erikson, E. H. (1968). *Identity, youth, and crisis.* New York: Norton.

Felmlee, D. H. (1999). Social norms in same- and cross-gender friendships. *Social Psychology Quarterly, 62*(1), 53–67.

Feuer, M., Towne, L., & Shavelson R. J. (2002). Scientific research and education. *Educational Researcher, 31*(8), 4–14.

Finn, J. D., & Achilles, C. (1990). Answers and questions about class size: A statewide experiment. *American Educational Research Journal, 27*(3), 557–577.

Finn, J. D., & Achilles, C. (1999). Tennessee's class size study: Findings, implications, and misconceptions. *Educational Evaluation and Policy Analysis, 21*(2), 97–109.

Firestone, W. A. (1985). The study of loose coupling: Problems, progress, and prospects. In A. C. Kerckhoff (Ed.), *Research in sociology of education and socialization* (Vol. 5, pp. 3–30). Greenwich, CT: JAI Press.

Fish, S. (2003). Truth but no consequences: Why philosophy doesn't matter. *Critical Inquiry, 29*(3), 389–417.

Fisher, R. A. (1935). *The design of experiments.* Edinburgh, UK: Oliver & Boyd.

Foster, E. M., & Fang, G. Y. (2004). Alternative methods for handling attrition: An illustration using data from the Fast Track evaluation. *Evaluation Review, 28*(5), 434–464.

Frangakis, C. E., & Rubin, D. B. (1999). Addressing complications of intention-to-treat analysis in the combined presence of all-or-none treatment-noncompliance and subsequent missing outcomes. *Biometrika, 86,* 365–379.

Gamoran, A. (1989). Measuring curriculum differentiation. *American Journal of Education, 97,* 129–143.

Gamoran, A., & Berends M. (1988). The effects of stratification in secondary schools: Synthesis of survey and ethnographic research. *Review of Educational Research, 57,* 415–435.

Gee, J. P. (2005). It's theories all the way down: A response to *Scientific Research in Education. Teachers College Record, 107*(1), 10–18.

Giangreco, M.F., & Taylor, S.J. (2003). "Scientifically based research" and qualitative inquiry. *Research and Practice for Persons with Severe Disabilities, 28*(3), 133–137.

Giordano, P. (2003). Relationships in adolescence. *Annual Review of Sociology, 29*, 257–281.

Granic, I., & Dishion, T. (2003). Deviant talk in adolescent friendships: A step toward measuring a pathogenic attractor process. *Social Development, 12*(3), 314–334.

Greenwald, R., Hedges, L.V., & Laine, R.D. (1996). The effect of school resources on student achievement. *Review of Educational Research, 66*, 361–396.

Hahn, J., Todd, P., & Van der Klaauw. (1999). *Evaluating the effect of an antidiscrimination law using a regression-discontinuity design* (Brief No. 7131). Cambridge, MA: National Bureau of Economic Research.

Hahn, J., Todd, P., & Van der Klaauw. (2001). Identification and estimation of treatment effects with a regression-discontinuity design. *Econometrica, 69*(1), 201–209.

Hallinan, S., & Williams, R. (1990). Students' characteristics and the peer-influence process. *Sociology of Education, 63*, 122–132.

Halpern, S.D., Karlawish, J.H., & Berlin, J.A. (2002). The continuing unethical conduct of underpowered clinical trials. *Journal of the American Medical Association, 288*, 358–362.

Hanushek, E.A. (1986). The economics of schooling: Production and efficiency in public schools. *Journal of Economic Literature, 24*, 1141–1177.

Heckman J.J. (1976). The common structure of statistical models of truncation, sample selection and limited dependent variables and a simple estimator for such models. *Annals of Economic and Social Measurement, 5*, 475–492.

Heckman, J.J. (1979). Sample selection bias as a specification error. *Econometrica, 47*(1), 153–161.

Hedberg, E. C., Santana, R., & Hedges, L. V. (2004, April). *The variance structure of academic achievement in America.* Paper presented at the annual meeting of the American Educational Research Association, San Diego, CA.

Hedges, L. V. (2004). Examining the effects of school organization on student achievement. In M. Ross (Ed.), *Instructional performance consequences of high poverty schooling.* Washington, DC: U.S. Government Printing Office.

Hedges, L. V. (2006). *Fixed effects versus mixed effects models.* Manuscript in preparation.

Higginbotham, H. N., West, S. G., & Forsyth, D. R. (1988). *Psychotherapy and behavior change: Social, cultural, and methodological perspectives.* New York: Pergamon.

Hirano, K., Imbens, G., Rider, G., & Rubin, D. B. (2001). Combining panel data sets with attrition and refreshment samples. *Econometrica, 69*(6), 1645–1659.

Holland, P. W. (1986). Statistics and causal inference. *Journal of the American Statistics Association, 81,* 945–970.

Holland, P. W. (1988). Causal inference, path analysis, and recursive structural equations models. In C. Clogg (Ed.), *Sociological methodology* (pp. 449–484). Washington, DC: American Sociological Association.

Holland, P. W., & Rubin, D. B. (1983). On Lord's Paradox. In H. Wainer & S. Messick, (Eds.), *Principals of modern psychological measurement* (pp. 3–25). Hillsdale, NJ: Lawrence Erlbaum.

Holmes, C. T. (1989). Grade-level retention effects: A meta-analysis of research studies. In L. A. Shepard & M. L. Smith (Eds.), *Flunking grades: Research and policies on retention* (pp. 16–33). Philadelphia: Falmer.

Hong, G., & Raudenbush, S. W. (2005). Effects of kindergarten retention policy on children's cognitive growth in reading and mathematics. *Educational Evaluation and Policy Analysis, 27*(3), 205–224.

Horner, R. H., Carr, E. G., Halle, J., McGee, G., Odom, S., & Wolery, M. (2005). The use of single-subject research to identify evidence-based practice in special education. *Exceptional Children, 71*(2), 165–179.

Imbens, G., & Rubin, D. B. (1997). Bayesian inference for causal effects in randomized experiments with noncompliance. *Annals of Statistics, 25,* 305–327.

Ingersoll, R. (1993). Loosely coupled organizations revisited. *Research in the Sociology of Organizations, 11,* 81–112.

Jackson, G. B. (1975). The research evidence on the effect of grade retention. *Review of Educational Research, 45*(3), 613–635.

Jacob, B., & Lefgren, L. (2004). Remedial education and student achievement: A regression discontinuity analysis. *Review of Economics and Statistics, 86*(1), 226–244.

Jimerson, S. R. (2001). Meta-analysis of grade retention research: Implications for practice in the 21st century. *School Psychology Review, 30,* 313–330.

Jurs, S. G., & Glass, G. V. (1971). Experimental mortality. *Journal of Experimental Education, 40,* 62–66.

Kaestle, C. F. (1993). The awful reputation of educational research. *Educational Researcher, 22,* 23–31.

Kamil, M. L. (2004). The current state of quantitative research. *Reading Research Quarterly, 39*(1), 100–107.

Karweit, N. L. (1992). Retention policy. In M. Alkin (Ed.), *Encyclopedia of educational research* (pp. 114–118). New York: Macmillan.

Kellam, S. G., & Langevin, D. J. (2003). A framework for understanding "evidence" in prevention research and programs. *Prevention Science, 4*(3), 137–153.

Kellam, S. G., Ling, X., Merisca, R., Brown, C. H., & Ialongo, N. (1998). The effect and level of aggression in the first grade classroom on the course and malleability of aggressive behavior into middle school. *Development and Psychopathology, 10*(2), 165–185.

Kellam, S. G., & Van Horn, Y. V. (1997). Life course development, community epidemiology, and preventive trials: A scientific structure for prevention research. *American Journal of Community Psychology, 25*(2), 177–187.

Kempthorne, O. (1952). *Design and analysis of experiments*. New York: Wiley.

Kilgore, S. B. (1991). The organizational context of tracking in schools. *American Journal of Sociology, 56*(2), 189–203.

Kilgore, S. B., & Pendleton, W. W. (1993). The organizational context of learning: A framework for understanding the acquisition of knowledge. *Sociology of Education, 66*(1), 63–87.

King, G., Honaker, J., Joseph, A., & Scheve, K. (2001). Analyzing incomplete political science data: An alternative algorithm for multiple imputation. *American Political Science Review, 95*, 49–69.

Kish L. (1987). *Statistical design for research*. New York: John Wiley and Sons.

Krei, M. S. (1998). Intensifying the barriers: The problem of inequitable teacher allocation in low-income urban schools. *Urban Education, 33*, 71–94.

Krueger, A. B. (1999). Experimental estimates of education production functions. *Quarterly Journal of Economics, 114*(2), 497–532.

Lagemann, E. C. (1999). An auspicious moment for education research? In E. C. Lagemann & L. S. Shulman (Eds.), *Issues in education research: Problems and possibilities* (pp. 3–16). San Francisco: Jossey-Bass.

Lagemann, E. C. (2000). *An elusive science: The troubling history of education research*. Chicago: University of Chicago Press.

Lagemann, E. C. (2005). Does history matter in education research? A brief for the humanities in the age of science. *Harvard Educational Review, 75*(1), 3–19.

Langford, H., Loeb, S., & Wyckoff, J. (2002). Teacher sorting and the plight of urban schools: A descriptive analysis. *Educational Evaluation and Policy Analysis, 24,* 37–62.

Lather, P. (2004). Scientific research in education: A critical perspective. *British Educational Research Journal, 30*(6), 759–772.

Lee, J. D. (2002). More than ability: Gender and personal relationships influence science and technology development. *Sociology of Education, 75,* 349–373.

Lee, V., & Bryk, A. (1986). The effects of single-sex secondary schools on students' achievement and attitudes. *Journal of Educational Psychology, 78,* 381–396.

Lee, V. E., Smith, J. B., & Croninger, R. G. (1997). How high school organization influences the equitable distribution of learning in math and science. *Sociology of Education, 70*(2), 128–150.

Leinhardt, G. (1980). Transition rooms: Promoting maturation or reducing education? *Journal of Education Psychology, 72,* 55–61.

Levin, J. R. (2003). Random thoughts on the (in)credibility of educational-psychological intervention research. *Educational Psychologist, 39*(3), 173–184.

Levin, J. R., & O'Donnell, A. M. (1999). What to do about educational research's credibility gaps? *Issues in Education, 5*(2), 177–229.

Lin, D. Y., Psaty, B. M., & Kronmal, R. A. (1998). Assessing the sensitivity of regression results to unmeasured confounders in observational studies. *Biometrics, 54,* 948–963.

Little, R. J., & Rubin, D. B. (2002). *Statistical analyses with missing data.* New York: John Wiley.

Little, R. J., & Yau, L. H. Y. (1998). Statistical techniques for analyzing data from preventive trials: Treatment of no-shows using Rubin's causal model. *Psychological Methods, 3,* 147–159.

Locke, J. (1975). *An essay concerning human understanding.* Oxford, UK: Clarendon Press. (Original work published in 1690)

Matsueda, R., & Anderson, K. (1998). The dynamics of delinquent peers and delinquent behavior. *Criminology, 36,* 269–308.

Mayer, R. E. (2003). Learning environments: The case for evidence-based practice and issue-driven research. *Educational Psychology Review, 15*(4), 359–366.

McCarthy, B., Felmlee, D., & Haga, J. (2004). Girl friends are better: Gender, friends, and crime among school and street youth. *Criminology, 42*(4), 805–835.

McDonald, S.-K., Keesler, V., Kauffman, N., & Schneider, B. (2006). Scaling-up exemplary interventions. *Educational Researcher, 35*(3), 15–24.

McKnight, C. C., Crosswhite, F. J., Dossey, J. A., Kifer, E., Swafford, J. O., Travers, K. J., et al. (1987). *The underachieving curriculum: Assessing U.S. school mathematics from an international perspective.* Champaign, IL: Stipes Publishing Company.

Morgan, S. L. (2001). Counterfactuals, causal effect heterogeneity, and the Catholic school effect on learning. *Sociology of Education, 74,* 341–374.

Morrison, F. J., Griffith, E. M., & Alberts, D. M. (1997). Nature-nurture in the classroom: Entrance age, school readiness, and learning in children. *Developmental Psychology, 33*(2), 254–262.

Moss, P. (2005). Toward "epistemic reflexivity" in educational research: A response to *Scientific Research in Education. Teachers College Record, 107*(1), 19–29.

Nagaoka, J., & Roderick, M. (2004). *Ending social promotion: The effects of retention.* Chicago: Consortium on Chicago School Research.

National Research Council. (2002). *Scientific research in education.* Washington, DC: National Academy Press.

National Research Council. (2004a). *Advancing scientific research in education.* Washington, DC: National Academy Press.

National Research Council. (2004b). *Implementing randomized field trials in education: Report of a workshop.* Washington, DC: National Academies Press.

National Science Foundation. (2004). *Final report on the National Science Foundation mathematics education portfolio review.* Washington, DC: National Science Foundation.

Neyman, J. (1923). On the application of probability theory to agricultural experiments: Essay on principles (D. M. Dabrowska & T. P. Speed, Trans.). *Statistical Sciences, 5,* 472–480.

Neyman, J. (1935). Statistical problems in agricultural experimentation. *Journal of the Royal Statistical Society, 2,* 107–180.

No Child Left Behind Act of 2001, Pub. L. No. 107-11, 115 Stat. 1425 (2002).

Norman, G. R., & Streiner, D. L. (2004). *PDQ statistics* (3rd ed.). Hamilton, Ontario, Canada: B. C. Decker.

Nye, B., Konstantopoulos, S., & Hedges, L. V. (2000). Effects of small classes on academic achievement: The results of the Tennessee class size experiment. *American Educational Research Journal, 37,* 123–151.

Nye, B., Konstantopoulos, S., & Hedges, L. V. (2004). How large are teacher effects? *Educational Evaluation and Policy Analysis, 26,* 237–257.

Plummer, D. L., & Graziano, W. G. (1987). Impact of grade retention on the social development of elementary school children. *Developmental Psychology, 23*(2), 267–275.

Popkewitz, T. S. (2004). Is the National Research Council Committee's report on *Scientific Research in Education* scientific? On trusting the manifesto. *Qualitative Inquiry, 10*(1), 62–78.

Raudenbush, S. W. (1997). Statistical analysis and optimal design for cluster randomized trials. *Psychological Methods, 2*(2), 173–185.

Raudenbush, S. W. (2005). Learning from attempts to improve schooling: The contribution of methodological diversity. *Educational Researcher, 34*(5), 25–31.

Raudenbush, S. W., Fotiu, R. P., & Cheong, Y. F. (1998). Inequality of access to educational resources: A national report card for eighth-grade math. *Educational Evaluation and Policy Analysis, 20*(4), 253–267.

Raudenbush, S. W., & Liu, X. (2000). Statistical power and optimal design for multisite randomized trials. *Psychological Methods, 5*(2), 199–213.

Reynolds, A. J. (1992). Grade retention and school adjustment: An explanatory analysis. *Educational Evaluation and Policy Analysis, 14*(2), 101–121.

Riegle-Crumb, C., Farkas, G., & Muller, C. (2006). The role of gender and friendship in advanced course-taking. *Sociology of Education, 79*(3), 206–228.

Rivkin, S. G., Hanushek, E. A., & Kain, J. F. (2005). Teachers, schools, and academic achievement. *Econometrica, 72*(3), 417–458.

Rosenbaum, P. R. (1986). Dropping out of high school in the United States: An observational study. *Journal of Educational Statistics, 11*(3), 207–224.

Rosenbaum, P. R. (2002). *Observational studies* (2nd ed.). New York: Springer.

Rosenbaum, P. R., & Rubin, D. B. (1983). The central role of the propensity score in observational studies for causal effects. *Biometrika, 70*(1), 41–55.

Rossi, J. S. (1990). Statistical power of psychological research: What have we gained in 20 years? *Journal of Consulting and Clinical Psychology, 58,* 646–656.

Rover, D. T. (2005). Centered on education [Review of the book *Scientific research in education*]. *Journal of Engineering Education, 94*(1), 195–197.

Rubin, D. B. (1974). Estimating causal effects of treatments in randomized and nonrandomized studies. *Journal of Educational Psychology, 66*, 688–701.

Rubin, D. B. (1977). Assignment of treatment group on the basis of a covariate. *Journal of Educational Statistics, 2*, 1–26.

Rubin, D. B. (1978). Bayesian inference for causal effects: The role of randomization. *Annals of Statistics, 6*, 34–58.

Rubin, D. B. (1980). Discussion of "Randomization analysis of experimental data in the Fisher randomization test" by Basu. *Journal of the American Statistical Association, 75*, 591–593.

Rubin, D. B. (1986). Which ifs have causal answers? Discussion of "Statistics and causal inference" by Holland. *Journal of the American Statistical Association, 81*, 961–962.

Rubin, D. B. (1997). Estimating causal effects from large data sets using propensity scores. *Annals of Internal Medicine, 127*(8), 757–763.

Rubin, D. B. (1998). More powerful randomization-based *p*-values in double-blind trials with noncompliance (with discussion). *Statistics in Medicine, 17*, 371–389.

Rubin, D. B. (2006). *Matched sampling for causal effects.* New York: Cambridge University Press.

Schmidt, W. H., McKnight, C., Cogan, L. S., Jakwerth, P. M., & Houang, R. T. (1999). *Facing the consequences: Using TIMSS for a closer look at U.S. mathematics and science education.* Dordrecht/Boston/London: Kluwer.

Schmidt, W. H., McKnight, C. C., Houang, R. T., Wang, H., Wiley, D. E., Cogan, L. S., et al. (2001). *Why schools matter: A cross-national comparison of curriculum and learning.* New York: John Wiley & Sons.

Schneider, B., Kertcher, Z., & Offer, S. (2006). Global trends towards education and science: Tension and resistance. In J. Ozga, T. Seddon, & T. Popkewitz (Eds.), *Education research and policy: Steering the knowledge-based economy* (pp. 200–215). New York: Routledge.

Schneider, B., & McDonald, S.-K. (Eds.). (2007a). *Scale-up in education: Vol. 1. Ideas in principle.* Lanham, MD: Rowman & Littlefield.

Schneider, B., & McDonald, S.-K. (Eds.). (2007b). *Scale-up in education: Vol. 2. Issues in practice.* Lanham, MD: Rowman & Littlefield.

Schneider, B., McDonald, S.-K., Brown, K. B., Schalliol, D., Makela, S., Yamaguchi, K., et al. (2006). *Evaluating the efficacy of the Center for Education at the National Academies: Report to the Center for Education.* Chicago: University of Chicago.

Schneider, B., & Stevenson, D. (1999). *The ambitious generation: America's teenagers, motivated but directionless.* New Haven, CT: Yale University Press.

Scientific research in education. (2002). Special issue of *Educational Researcher, 31*(8).

Scientific research in education. (2005). Special issue of *Teachers College Record, 107*(1).

Secretary of Education. (2005, January 25). Scientifically based evaluation methods (RIN 1890–ZA00). *Federal Register, 70*(15), 3586.

Seymour, E., & Hewitt, N. (1997). *Talking about leaving: Why undergraduates leave the sciences.* Boulder, CO: Westview Press.

Shadish, W. R., Cook, T. D., & Campbell, D. T. (2002). *Experimental and quasi-experimental designs for generalized causal inference.* Boston: Houghton Mifflin.

Shapka, J. D., & Keating, D. P. (2003). Effects of a girls-only curriculum during adolescence: Performance, persistence, and engagement in mathematics and science. *American Educational Research Journal, 40,* 929–960.

Shavelson, R. J., & Berliner, D. C. (1988). Erosion of the education research infrastructure. *Educational Researcher, 17*(1), 9–12.

Shepard, L. A. (1989). A review of research on kindergarten retention. In L. A. Shepard & M. L. Smith (Eds.), *Flunking grades: Research and policies on retention* (pp. 64–78). London: Falmer Press.

Shu, X., & Marini, M. M. (1998). Gender-related change in occupational aspirations. Sociology of Education, 71(1), 43–67.

Slavin, R. E., & Madden, N. A. (2001). *One million children: Success for All*. Thousand Oaks, CA: Corwin.

Slavin, R. E., Madden, N. A., Dolan, L. J., Wasik, B. A., Ross, S. M., & Smith, L. M. (1994). "Whenever and wherever we choose": The replication of Success for All. *Phi Delta Kappan, 75*, 639–647.

Slavin, R. E., Madden, N. A., Karweit, N. L., Dolan, L., & Wasik, B. A. (1992). *Success for All: A relentless approach to prevention and early intervention in elementary schools*. Arlington, VA: Educational Research Service.

Smith, M. L., & Shephard, L. A. (1988). Kindergarten readiness and retention: A qualitative study of teachers' beliefs and practices. *American Educational Research Journal, 25*(3), 307–333.

Sorenson, A. B. (1970). Organizational differentiation of students and educational opportunity. *Sociology of Education, 43*(4), 355–376.

Sorenson, A. B. (1987). The organization and differentiation of students in schools as an opportunity structure. In M. T. Hallinan (Ed.), *The social organization of schools*. New York: Plenum Press.

South, S., & Haynie, D. (2004). Friendship networks of mobile adolescents. *Social Forces, 83*, 315–350.

Spooner, F., & Browder, D. M. (2003). Scientifically-based research in education and students with low incidence disabilities. *Research in Practice for Persons With Severe Disabilities, 28*(3), 177–125.

Sroufe, G. E. (1997). Improving the "awful reputation" of education research. *Educational Researcher, 26*(7), 26–28.

Staiger, D., & Stock, J. (1997). Instrumental variables regression with weak instruments. *Econometrica, 65*, 557–587.

Stake, J., & Nicken, S. (2005). Adolescent girls' and boys' science peer relationships and perceptions of the possible self as scientist. *Sex Roles, 52*, 1–11.

Stevenson, D. L., Schiller, K. S., & Schneider, B. (1994). Sequences of opportunities of learning. *Sociology of Education, 67*(3), 184–198.

Stoiber, K. C. (2002). Revisiting efforts on constructing a knowledge base of evidence-based intervention within school psychology. *School Psychology Quarterly, 17*(4), 533–546.

Stolzenberg, R. M., & Relles, D. A. (1997). Tools for intuition about sample selection bias and its correction. *American Sociological Review, 62*(3), 494–507.

Tanner, C. K., & Gallis, S. A. (1997). Student retention: Why is there a gap between the majority of research findings and school practice? *Psychology in the Schools, 34*(2), 107–114.

Thompson, B., Diamond, K. E., McWilliam, R., Snyder, P., & Snyder, S. W. (2005). Evaluating the quality of evidence from correlational research for evidence-based practice. *Exceptional Children, 71*(2), 181–194.

Van der Klaauw, W. (2002). Estimating the effect of financial aid offers on college enrollment: A regression-discontinuity approach. *International Economic Review, 43*(4), 1249–1287.

Warr, M. (1993). Parents, peers, and delinquency. *Social Forces, 72*(1), 247–264.

Weermand, F., & Smeenk, W. (2005). Peer similarity in delinquency for different types of friends: A comparison using two measurement methods. *Criminology, 43*(2), 499–523.

Weiss, C. H. (1999). Research-policy linkages: How much influence does social science research have? In *UNESCO, World Social Science Report 1999* (pp. 194–205). Paris: UNESCO/Elsevier.

West, S. G., Biesanz, J. C., & Pitts, S. C. (2000). Causal inference and generalization in field settings. In H. T. Reis & C. M. Judd (Eds.), *Handbook of research methods in social and personality psychology* (pp. 40–84). Cambridge, UK: Cambridge University Press.

Whiteley, B. J., Seelig, S. E., Weinshenker, M., & Schneider, B. (2002). *The AERA research grants program: Key findings of selected studies* (A report to the AERA Grants Board). Chicago: University of Chicago and NORC, Academic Research Centers.

Willinksky, J. (2005). Scientific research in a democratic culture: Or, What's a social science for? *Teachers College Record, 107*(1), 38–51.

Winship, C., & Mare, R. D. (1992). Models for sample selection bias. *Annual Review of Sociology, 18,* 327–350.

Winship, C., & Morgan, S. L. (1999). The estimation of causal effects from observational data. *Annual Review of Sociology, 25,* 659–706.

Xie, Y., & Shauman, K. (2003). *Women in science: Career processes and outcomes.* Cambridge, MA: Harvard University Press.

Biographical Sketches

Barbara Schneider is the John A. Hannah University Distinguished Chair in the College of Education and the Department of Sociology at Michigan University. Her work focuses on the study of adolescent transitions and the social contexts, primarily the family and the school, which influence the path to adulthood. She is also the principal investigator of the Data Research and Development Center, which is devoted to studying how to bring promising educational interventions to scale. Her publications include *The Ambitious Generation: America's Teenagers Motivated but Directionless* (co-authored with David Stevenson; Yale University Press, 2000), *Trust in Schools: A Core Resource for Improvement* (co-authored with Anthony S. Bryk; Russell Sage, 2002), and *Being Together, Working Apart: Dual Career Families and the Work-Life Balance* (co-edited with Linda Waite; Cambridge University Press, 2005).

Martin Carnoy is Vida Jacks Professor of Education at Stanford University. His research focuses on the economic value of education, the underlying political economy of educational policy, and the financing and resource allocation aspects of educational production. Much of his work is comparative and international and investigates the impact of global economic and social change on the value of education and the way educational systems are organized. An example of this is his book *Sustaining the New Economy: Work, Family and Community in the Information Age* (Harvard University Press, 2000). He is currently researching the impact on educational quality of large-scale interventions such as the privatization of education, administrative decentralization, and education accountability reforms both in the United States and in developing countries. He has published a number of articles and books based on this research, including *Cuba's Academic Advantage*, forthcoming from Stanford University Press in 2007, which compares the effectiveness of educational systems in various Latin American countries. His policy work is currently focused on the labor market for teachers across countries and how teachers' relative remuneration and status are related to students' performance on international tests.

Jeremy Kilpatrick is Regents Professor of Mathematics Education at the University of Georgia. His research interests include teachers' proficiency in teaching mathematics, mathematics curriculum change and its history, mathematics assessment, and the history of research in mathematics education. His edited publications include *A Research Companion to Principles and Standards for School Mathematics* (with W. Gary Martin and Deborah Schifter) and *A History of School Mathematics* (with George Stanic), both published by the National Council of Teachers of Mathematics in 2003. Kilpatrick chaired the Committee on Mathematics Learning of the National Research Council, whose report *Adding It Up: Helping Children Learn Mathematics* was published by the National Academies Press in 2001. He also served on the RAND Mathematics Study Panel, whose report *Mathematical Proficiency for All Students: Toward a Strategic Research and Development Program in Mathematics Education*, published by the RAND Corporation, appeared in 2002. Both reports address the development of proficiency in teaching mathematics by improving teachers' knowledge, skill, and practice. Strengthening the professional education of mathematics teachers is the aim of the NSF-funded Center for Proficiency in Teaching Mathematics, in which Kilpatrick serves as a principal investigator.

William H. Schmidt is the University Distinguished Professor at Michigan State University in the College of Education and is currently co-director of the Education Policy Center, co-director of the U.S. China Center for Research, and co-director of the NSF PROM/SE project and holds faculty appointments in the Departments of Educational Psychology and Statistics. Previously he served as National Research Coordinator and Executive Director of the U.S. National Center which oversaw participation of the United States in the IEA-sponsored Third International Mathematics and Science Study (TIMSS). In 2006, Schmidt was elected to the National Academy of Education. His current writing and research concerns issues of academic content in K–12 schooling, assessment theory, and the effects of curriculum on academic achievement. He is also concerned with educational policy related to mathematics, science, and testing in general. He has published in numerous journals, including the *Journal of the American Statistical Association*, the *Journal of Educational Statistics*, and the *Journal of Educational Measurement*. He has co-authored seven books, including *Why Schools Matter* (2001, John Wiley & Sons).

Richard J. Shavelson is the Margaret Jack Professor of Education, a professor of psychology (courtesy), and a senior fellow in the Woods Institute for the Environment at Stanford University. His current work includes the assessment of science achievement and the study of inquiry-based science teaching and its impact on students' knowledge structures and performance. Other work includes studies of computer cognitive training on working memory, fluid intelligence and science achievement, assessment of undergraduates' learning with the Collegiate Learning Assessment, accountability in higher education, the scientific basis of education research, and new standards for measuring students' science achievement in the National Assessment of Educational Progress. His publications include *Statistical Reasoning for the Behavioral Sciences* (Allyn & Bacon, 1996), *Generalizability Theory: A Primer,* with Noreen Webb (Sage, 1991), and *Scientific Research in Education,* edited with Lisa Towne (National Academies Press, 2002). He is currently working on a book tentatively titled, *The Quest to Assess Learning and Hold Higher Education Accountable.*